WHAT EVERY PRINCIPAL SHOULD KNOW ABOUT

OPERATIONAL LEADERSHIP

WHAT EVERY PRINCIPAL SHOULD KNOW ABOUT LEADERSHIP
The 7-Book Collection

By Jeffrey Glanz

What Every Principal Should Know About Instructional Leadership

What Every Principal Should Know About Cultural Leadership

What Every Principal Should Know About Ethical and Spiritual Leadership

What Every Principal Should Know About School-Community Leadership

What Every Principal Should Know About Collaborative Leadership

What Every Principal Should Know About Operational Leadership

What Every Principal Should Know About Strategic Leadership

WHAT EVERY PRINCIPAL SHOULD KNOW ABOUT

OPERATIONAL LEADERSHIP

JEFFREY GLANZ

CORWIN PRESS
A SAGE Publications Company
Thousand Oaks, California

For information:

Corwin Press
A Sage Publications Company
2455 Teller Road
Thousand Oaks, California 91320
E-mail: order@corwinpress.com

Sage Publications Ltd.
1 Oliver's Yard
55 City Road
London EC1Y 1SP
United Kingdom

Sage Publications India Pvt. Ltd.
B-42, Panchsheel Enclave
Post Box 4109
New Delhi 110 017 India

Printed in the United States of America.

Library of Congress Cataloging-in-Publication Data

Glanz, Jeffrey.
What every principal should know about operational leadership / Jeffrey Glanz.
    p. cm.
Includes bibliographical references and index.
ISBN 1-4129-1591-0 (pbk.)
    1. School management and organization—Handbooks, manuals, etc.
2. School principals—Handbooks, manuals, etc. I. Title.
LB2805.G525 2006
371.2′012—dc22   2005022378

This book is printed on acid-free paper.

05   06   07   08   09   10   9   8   7   6   5   4   3   2   1

Acquisitions Editor:	Elizabeth Brenkus
Editorial Assistant:	Candice L. Ling
Project Editor:	Tracy Alpern
Copy Editor:	Rachel Hile Bassett
Proofreader:	Christine Dahlin
Typesetter:	C&M Digitals (P) Ltd.
Indexer:	Gloria Tierney
Cover Designer:	Rose Storey
Graphic Designer:	Scott Van Atta

Contents

To all principals who selflessly work through the mundane, yet essential, operational tasks that their job entails. Few realize the import of their work, but they know that operational leadership, done well, makes all the rest possible.

Acknowledgments

Instructional, cultural, collaborative, ethical-spiritual, school-community, and strategic leadership are all certainly important in our work. In other volumes in this groundbreaking principal leadership series, we have highlighted the importance of each of these forms of leadership. We realize that one is not necessarily more important than another. They all, indeed, need to be viewed as forming a unity of sorts. Yet, if I were asked which form of leadership is most fundamental, in that all the others are not possible without it, I would undoubtedly declare that a seventh form is most critical, and that is operational leadership. Dealing with organizational skills, facilities management, budget and finance, human resources issues, and the like are not the most exciting responsibilities we undertake, but they are critical, for without them all the rest would not be possible. Operational leadership, then, is the foundation for all other forms of leadership (see Figure 1 on page xiii). Good principals know this to be true. They work arduously to ensure that sound operational procedures are in place in their schools. This book and series are dedicated to all who aspire to the principalship, who currently serve as principals, or who have been principals and to all who believe in such work. No nobler enterprise or profession exists, for principals are the ones who establish and maintain conducive environments so that all people succeed in their school, and so that, most especially, conditions are set into motion that best facilitate student achievement.

* * * * * * * * * * * * * * * *

Thanks to Debby Sachs, Senior Grants Officer for Region 6, New York City Department of Education, for her materials and insights into the school budget process. Also, I learned much as

I was trained for the principalship in New York City under the mentorship of Dr. Thomas Montero and others in the Board of Education. I was exposed to many pieces of information that have become part of my knowledge base. If I inadvertently used some of this information without proper acknowledgment, please let me know so I may make corrections in future editions of this and other books in the series. Thanks to editor Lizzie Brenkus for guiding me through the process. Many thanks also go to Robb Clouse, editorial director, who prompted me to consider a trilogy of sorts: a book about teaching, which eventuated into *Teaching 101*; a book about assistant principals, which led to *The Assistant Principal's Handbook*; and a book about principals, which resulted, to my surprise, in this groundbreaking series, *What Every Principal Should Know About Leadership*.

Special thanks to my wife, Lisa, without whose support such a venture would be impossible. I love you . . . at least as much as I love writing.

Corwin Press gratefully acknowledges the contributions of the following individuals:

Kimberly Boelkes, Principal
Eastview Elementary School
Canton, IL

Michele Merkle, Principal
York Suburban High School
York, PA

Ann Porter, 2002 NAESP National Distinguished Principal
Lewis & Clark Elementary School
Grand Forks, ND

Paul Young, Former Principal, Executive Director
West After School Center
Lancaster, OH

About the Author

 **Jeffrey Glanz, EdD**, currently serves as Dean of Graduate Programs and Chair of the Department of Education at Wagner College in Staten Island, New York. He also coordinates the educational leadership program that leads to New York State certification as a principal or assistant principal. Prior to arriving at Wagner, he served as executive assistant to the president of Kean University in Union, New Jersey. Dr. Glanz held faculty status as a tenured professor in the Department of Instruction and Educational Leadership at Kean University's College of Education. He was named Graduate Teacher of the Year in 1999 by the Student Graduate Association and was also that year's recipient of the Presidential Award for Outstanding Scholarship. He served as an administrator and teacher in the New York City public schools for 20 years. Dr. Glanz has authored, coauthored, or coedited 13 books and has more than 35 peer-reviewed article publications. With Corwin Press he coauthored the bestselling *Supervision That Improves Teaching* (2nd ed.) and *Supervision in Practice: Three Steps to Improve Teaching and Learning* and authored *The Assistant Principal's Handbook* and *Teaching 101: Classroom Strategies for the Beginning Teacher.* More recently he coauthored *Building Effective Learning Communities: Strategies for Leadership, Learning, & Collaboration.* Most recently, Dr. Glanz has authored *What Every Principal Should Know About Leadership: The 7-Book Collection:*

What Every Principal Should Know About Instructional Leadership

What Every Principal Should Know About Cultural Leadership

What Every Principal Should Know About Ethical and Spiritual Leadership

What Every Principal Should Know About School-Community Leadership

What Every Principal Should Know About Collaborative Leadership

What Every Principal Should Know About Operational Leadership

What Every Principal Should Know About Strategic Leadership

Consult his Web site for additional information: http://www .wagner.edu/faculty/users/jglanz/web/.

* * * * * * * * * * * * * * * *

The "About the Author" information you've just glanced at (excuse the pun . . . my name? . . . Glanz, "glance"?!) is standard author bio info you find in most books. As you'll discover if you glance at . . . I mean *read* . . . the Introduction, I want this book to be user-friendly in several ways. One of the ways is that I want to write as I would converse with you in person. Therefore, I prefer in most places to use the first person, so please excuse the informality. Although we've likely never met, we really do know each other if you think about it. We share a common passion about leadership, school building leadership to be more precise. We share many similar experiences. In an experiential, almost spiritual, sense, we have much in common. What I write about directly relates, I hope, to your lived experience. The information in this volume, as with the entire series, is meant to resonate, stir, provoke, and provide ideas about principal leadership, which is vital in order to promote excellence and achievement for all.

This traditional section of a book is titled "About the Author." The first paragraph in this section tells you what I "do," not "about" me or who I am. I won't bore you with all details "about me," but I'd like just to share one bit of info that communicates more meaningfully about "me" than the information in the first paragraph. I am (I presume like you) passionate about what I do. I love to teach, guide, mentor, learn, supervise, and lead. For me, leadership is self-preservation. Personally and professionally,

I strive to do my very best, to use whatever God-given leadership talents I possess to make a difference in the lives of others. I continually strive to improve myself intellectually and socially, but also physically and spiritually. Operational leadership may be mundane, but I realize it's vital and critical to my success. I see myself as part of a larger community of learners as we share, experience, overcome difficulties, learn from our mistakes, and in the end help others (students, colleagues, and community members) achieve their educational goals.

If any of the information in this book series touches you in any way, please feel free to contact me by using my personal e-mail address: tora.dojo@verizon.net. I encourage you to share your reactions, comments, and suggestions, or simply to relate an anecdote or two, humorous or otherwise, that may serve as "information from the field" for future editions of this work, ultimately to help others. Your input is much appreciated.

Figure 1

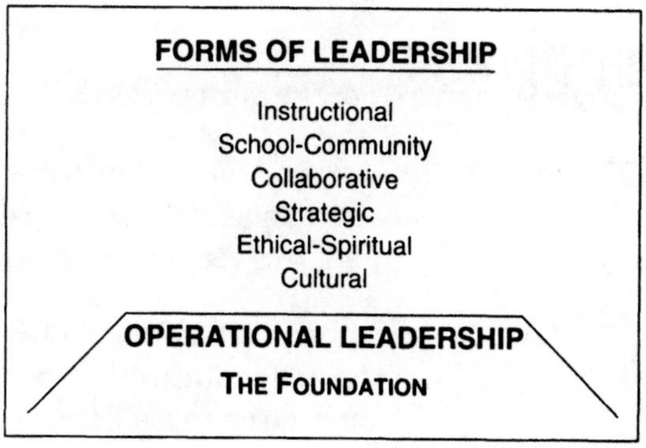

```
┌─────────────────────────────────────┐
│        FORMS OF LEADERSHIP          │
│                                     │
│            Instructional            │
│          School-Community           │
│             Collaborative           │
│               Strategic             │
│            Ethical-Spiritual        │
│               Cultural              │
│     ╱─────────────────────────╲     │
│    ╱  OPERATIONAL LEADERSHIP    ╲    │
│   ╱        THE FOUNDATION        ╲   │
└─────────────────────────────────────┘
```

Questionnaire: Before We Get Started . . .

Directions: Using the Likert scale on the next page, circle the answer that best represents your on-the-spot belief about each statement. The questionnaire serves as an advanced organizer of sorts for some of the key topics in this book, although items are purposely constructed in no particular order. Discussion of each topic, though, occurs within the context of relevant chapters. Responses or views to each statement are presented in a subsection following the questionnaire (this section begins "Now, let's analyze your responses . . ."). You may or may not agree with the points made, but I hope you will be encouraged to reflect on your own views. Reflective activities follow to allow for deeper analysis. Elaboration of ideas emanating from this brief activity will occur throughout the text and series. I encourage you to share reflections (yours and mine) with colleagues. I'd appreciate your personal feedback via the e-mail address I've listed in the "About the Author" section.

SA = Strongly Agree ("For the most part, yes.")
 A = Agree ("Yes, but . . .")
 D = Disagree ("No, but . . .")
SD = Strongly Disagree ("For the most part, no.")

SA   A   D   SD   1. Leading and managing are essential
                       requirements for the principalship, but
                       they address very different purposes.

SA   A   D   SD   2. I feel uncomfortable with theories
                       involving administration, because they
                       are often disconnected from practice.

SA   A   D   SD   3. Leadership is essentially a higher calling
                       than management.

SA   A   D   SD   4. Principals should attend to both the
                       operational and educational aspects of
                       the job with equal vigor and attention.

SA   A   D   SD   5. Research indicates that principals,
                       especially new ones, retain their jobs
                       because of their managerial role but would
                       rather delegate management functions to
                       others so that they could devote more time
                       to instructional leadership.

6. Examine the list of duties below that reflect some of the topics discussed in this book. First, rank them in terms of what you think you and your assistant principal(s) (APs) *actually* do in schools (i.e., award a #1 to the duty you think you or they do most frequently, #2 for the next most frequent duty, etc.). Second, rank them according to what is, in your view, their degree of importance (i.e., give a #1 to the duty principals and APs *should* be engaged in, a #2 to the next important duty, etc. Of course, your rankings may differ for APs). Compare your responses to the discussion in the answer section.

Student discipline

Lunch duty

School scheduling (coverages*)

Ordering textbooks

Parental conferences

Assemblies

Administrative duties

Articulation**

Evaluation of teachers

Student attendance

Emergency arrangements

Instructional media services

Counseling pupils

School clubs and the like

Assisting PTA

Formulating goals

Staff development (inservice)

Faculty meetings

Teacher training

Instructional leadership

Public relations

Curriculum development

Innovations and research

School budgeting

Teacher selection

*Coverages refer to scheduling substitute teachers to cover for absent regular classroom teachers.

**Articulation refers to the administrative and logistical duties required to prepare for graduation (e.g., preparing and sending cumulative record cards for graduating fifth graders to the middle school).

Before we analyze your responses, consider the importance of operational leadership. Running a school takes much effort, determination, and skill. As an operational leader you:

- Organize all school activities
- Establish widely known and accepted procedures for conducting business
- Coordinate programs and training activities
- Evaluate programs and personnel
- Prepare and oversee school and program schedules
- Manage physical plant and facilities
- Work closely with custodial, cafeteria, and office staff
- Prepare financial reports
- Assume responsibility for fiscal and budgetary integrity
- Recruit teachers
- Monitor teacher induction and mentoring
- Communicate

As you consider these responsibilities and many related others, share your thoughts about these questions with a colleague:

Reflective Questions

1. Do you really believe operational leadership is essential to your work as principal? How so? Be specific.

2. How much time would you devote to such responsibilities? With all that you do administratively, how would you find the time to engage in other forms of leadership (see Figure 1 on page xiii)?

3. How do you plan on delegating authority?

4. How do you react to a principal colleague who laments, "It's virtually impossible to really lead my school when I am so bogged down in administrivia?"

5. Identify principals you know or have known. How have they balanced their leadership responsibilities? What can you learn from them?

6. React to this statement: "As principal I am most fundamentally an organizer of operations. I establish a conducive learning community or environment that is safe, secure, and organized so that others may successfully engage in instructional and collaborative leadership." Do you agree or disagree with this statement? Explain.

* * * * * * * * * * * * * * * *

Examine these quotations about operational leadership. What do they mean to you?

"The choice is not whether a principal is leader or manager but whether the two emphases are in balance and, indeed, whether they complement each other."

—Thomas J. Sergiovanni

"Measures must focus attention on elements of systems that people believe can make a difference in the results toward which the system is managed."

—Phillip C. Schlechty

"Educational administrators are frequently expected to take on the roles of educational superperson, technical manager, and democratic leader."

—Cherry A. McGee Banks

"Leaders are people who do the right thing; managers are people who do things right."

—Warren Bennis

"Management is problem-oriented. Leadership is opportunity-oriented. Management works the system. Leadership works on the system."

—Stephen Covey

"Management is about human beings. Its task is to make people capable of joint performance, to make their strengths effective and their weaknesses irrelevant."

—Peter Drucker

"The principal is ultimately responsible for almost everything that happens in school and out."

—Roland S. Barth

"Leadership literature frequently gives the impression that managerial functions or responsibilities are less important than the leadership functions or responsibilities. Principals usually want to be instructional leaders. However, management and leadership responsibilities go hand in hand."

—Harvey B. Alvy and Pam Robbins

* * * * * * * * * * * * * * * *

Now, let's analyze your responses to the questionnaire:

1. Leading and managing are essential requirements for the principalship, but they address very different purposes.

Principals must exhibit leadership qualities, but at the same time they must serve as efficient managers. Leading without managing well will eventuate in failure; the converse is also true. A leading authority on the subject, Peter Northouse (1997), explains that leadership is a process similar to management. Both processes or functions involve influencing others, working with people, and goal accomplishment.

Significant differences, however, are readily apparent. Emerging from the industrial era, management aims to produce order and consistency in the workplace. Reducing chaos and enhancing efficiency are prime objectives. Organizational theorists such as Fayol (1916) identify the following management activities still relevant today: planning, organizing, staffing, and controlling. Leadership, in contrast, emphasizes the importance of change, vision, motivation, and the like. Northouse contrasts the two processes as follows:

> *In planning and budgeting, the emphasis of management is on establishing detailed agendas, setting timetables, . . . allocating the necessary resources to meet organizational objectives. In contrast to this, the emphasis of leadership is on direction setting, clarifying the big picture, building a vision that is often long term, and setting strategy to create needed organizational changes. (p. 8)*

Still, Northouse (1997) concludes that "Although there are clear differences between management and leadership, or leaders and managers, there is a considerable amount of overlap" (p. 9).

More precisely, leading and managing should be viewed as two sides of the same coin. Managing (i.e., dealing with standard operational procedures; overseeing transportation, scheduling, human resource management, etc.) is critical so that you can take leadership initiatives. To run a school you need both functions. Yet you must realize that clear differences exist, as will be evident as you continue reading. When it comes to leading and managing, Kaser, Mundry, Loucks-Horsley, and Stiles (2002) explain that "One of the major contributions that a leader can make is to always be able to distinguish between these two important functions" (p. 10).

Reflective Question

1. In what ways have you seen principals manage? Lead? Describe in detail.

---

2. I feel uncomfortable with theories involving administration, because they are often disconnected from practice.

Kurt Lewin once said, and I paraphrase, there is nothing as practical as good theory. Noted behavioral researcher and theorist Fred Kerlinger (1986) once posited that theory is "a set of interrelated constructs (concepts), definitions, and propositions that present a systematic view of phenomena by specifying relations among variables with a purpose of explaining and predicting phenomena" (p. 9). Implied in Kerlinger's definition of a theory is a connection to practice. Theories, at their best, inform practice, as good practice should reflect and inform theory. Lunenburg and Ornstein (1996) confirm administrators' discomfort with theory but then point to the benefits of theory:

> *Many school administrators feel uncomfortable with theories. They prefer that social scientists provide them with practical prescriptions for administering their schools. Upon closer examination, however, almost every action a school administrator takes is based to some degree on a theory. For example, a school administrator may include subordinates in a decision involving an issue that is relevant to them and that they have the expertise to make, instead of making the decision unilaterally. This choice is made because including subordinates in decisions, which pass the test of relevance and expertise, will likely increase their commitment to carry out the decision once it is made. Without realizing it, the school administrator made this choice on the basis of a theory.*
>
> *Educational administrators would most likely flounder without theories to guide them in making choices. Thus, theories provide a guiding framework for understanding, predicting, and controlling behavior in organizations. Theories also contribute to the advancement of knowledge in the field. (p. 3)*

Three major theories of administration that are important for a principal to know include classical organizational theories, human relations theories, and behavioral science theories. The charts that follow summarize major points of each theory and can perhaps serve as a reminder if you've taken a graduate course in, say, administration and supervision.

I. Classical Organizational Theories

1. Scientific Management

Era	Theorist(s)	Theme	Major principles	Ultimate goal
1900–1910	Fredrick Taylor	Managers must study work scientifically to produce efficient workers (emphasis on workers; focus on technical skills of managers).	A. Scientific job analysis—Find one best way of performing a task. B. Selection of personnel—Train workers to perform task. C. Management cooperation—Managers should cooperate with workers to ensure efficiency. D. Functional supervising—Managers oversee workers.	To maximize work productivity

2. Administration Management

Era	Theorist(s)	Theme	Major principles	Ultimate goal
1910–1925	Henri Fayol Luther Gulick Max Weber	Managers ensure efficiency of management of entire organization (focus on organization, not only individual).	1. Fayol Fayol's five basic functions of management A. Planning B. Organization C. Commanding D. Coordinating E. Controlling	To ensure work efficiency

(Continued)

(Continued)

Era	Theorist(s)	Theme	Major principles	Ultimate goal
			Fayol's 14 principles of management A. Division of work B. Authority C. Discipline D. Unity of command E. Unity of direction F. Subordination of individual interest G. Remuneration H. Centralization I. Scalar chain of command J. Order K. Equity L. Stability of personnel M. Initiative N. Esprit de corps 2. Gulick's seven functions of management A. Planning B. Organizing C. Staffing D. Directing E. Coordinating F. Reporting G. Budgeting 3. Weber's concept of bureaucracy as an "ideal" structure for organizational effectiveness (emphasizes division of labor, rules, and hierarchy of authority)	

Classical organizational theories have influenced practice in numerous ways, some positive and some not so positive.

Reflective Question

1. Can you name some positive and not-so-positive effects classical organizational theories have had on practice in schools?

Criticisms of the aforementioned theories led to the emergence of a second major theory of administration.

II. Human Relations Approach

Era	Theorist(s)	Theme	Major principles	Ultimate goal
1925–1940	Elton Mayo Kurt Lewin Carl Rogers	This theory emphasizes importance of attending to human (group) behavior and motivation to enhance individual performance (focus on human skills and management).	Mayo's Hawthorne studies; Lewin's group dynamics and work on demographic and authoritarian managers; Rogers's emphasis on the individual. All human relations approaches include seven assumptions: 1. People are motivated by social and psychological needs and external incentives.	To ensure that the needs of the individual are met

(Continued)

(Continued)

Era	Theorist(s)	Theme	Major principles	Ultimate goal
			2. People possess needs for security, belonging, and so on.	
			3. People's perceptions of reality in the workplace affect their behavior.	
			4. People develop formal and informal networks of support.	
			5. Individual and group behavior is influenced by many social factors.	
			6. People work better under supportive management styles.	
			7. Effective communication is central to a well-functioning organization.	

Reflective Question

1. How would you ensure that the needs of both the individual and the organization are met in your school? Isn't this impossible? Aren't most situations problematic, especially in cases where rules and policies of the organization must be ensured?

A third theory then emerged as an attempt to reconcile both theories.

III. Behavioral Science Approach

Era	Theorist(s)	Theme	Major principles	Ultimate goal
1940–1980s	Chester Barnard Chris Argyris Jacob Getzels and Egon Guba Abraham Maslow Douglas McGregor Fredrick Herzberg	This theory represents an attempt to combine classical organizational theory with human relations approaches. Manager must be an efficient technician and effective in relating to the individual. The goal is to harmonize individual interests with organizational necessities.	1. Barnard's cooperative system 2. Argyris's individual and organizational model 3. Getzels and Guba's nomothetic and idiographic theories 4. Maslow's need hierarchy 5. McGregor's Theory X and Theory Y 6. Herzberg's hygiene and motivation factor	To ensure that needs of both individual and organization are met

Over the past 30 years, many other theories have emerged from these three, most of which are an attempt to translate theories into practice. They represent ways of bridging theory with practice by creating school organizations that function to meet the academic and social needs of students (see, e.g., Bennis, 1990; Deming, 2000; Elmore, 1990; Hersey & Blanchard, 1992; Senge, 1990; Sergiovanni, 2000). Theories of administration and leadership have not only deepened our understanding of how schools as organizations work, but have contributed to improving practice by illustrating ways in which individuals within schools can reach their potential.

3. Leadership is essentially a higher calling than management.

The literature in the field of administration clearly distinguishes between leadership and management. This distinction implies that "leadership is a higher calling." "Successful new and veteran principals alike, however, view their managerial role as vital to their leadership responsibilities" (Alvy & Robbins, 2005, p. 52).

Underscoring the importance of management-related activities of a principal as connected to leadership responsibilities, Alvy and Robbins continue:

> *They exert leadership by ensuring that the school building is safe, maintaining bathrooms that are sanitary and free from graffiti, providing comfortable desks and chairs for students and teachers, maintaining adequate student instructional resources and teacher supplies, and having a sound understanding of the school budget. (p. 52)*

Alvy and Robbins (2005) explain that principals can easily undertake their management obligations and still exert leadership. For instance, they explain, as a principal is patrolling the hallways to "supervise students as they move between classes" he or she has a "wonderful opportunity to congratulate [a student] on his improved math score" or to ask another student "how her science fair project is coming along" (p. 52).

In the "old" days, a principal's role focused almost exclusively on managerial duties. A principal must indeed possess skills of organization, administration, and general management. Principals also need these skills today, but they must be combined with many other leadership responsibilities (e.g., instructional, cultural, strategic). It's not a matter of one being more or less important. As a principal today, you must view the two as complementary, that is, as working in unison for the benefit of all who work in schools.

4. Principals should attend to both the operational and educational aspects of the job with equal vigor and attention.

In an idealistic world of unlimited resources, the principalship might be divided into two separate roles or functionaries. One individual could have sole responsibility for the leadership functions of the position, while the other would be attentive to the managerial aspects. Without debating the merits of such a proposal, we certainly cannot afford the luxuries of even entertaining such a possibility in all schools in America. Clearly, too many economic, political, and other constraints exist for such a setup to take hold uniformly for all schools. Perhaps in the distant future, such a proposal might eventuate. The traditional role of principal has focused, however, on both the operational and educational aspects of the job. You were hired as principal with the expectation that you would manage school facilities and operations as well as serve as instructional, cultural, strategic, and collaborative leader. Principals today are certainly challenged by a more complex school environment than any other principal in the past faced. The requirements for the job are certainly awesome. Becoming a good manager and leader takes practice and experience. Fortunately, we have many fine examples of individuals who nobly serve as principals and perform both functions admirably.

Notwithstanding the foregoing, it doesn't necessarily mean that as principal you must attend to both functions equally. Attention to leadership (e.g., instructional) is imperative, and one cannot shirk responsibility in that area. However, one need not fully immerse oneself in all aspects of management. Delegation of authority and responsibility in management issues is highly suggested, even commendable. Following the lead of Drake and Roe (2003), I believe that "the principal's management technique . . . should be 'management by exception'; that is, routine matters should be handled by others who are responsible to the principal, and only special and exceptional matters should be referred to the principal" (p. 437). Attention to the managerial aspects of our job is imperative. But as principal, you are not merely a manager. Serving as a principal requires attention to both management and leadership. A principal only good at organizing and managing but not at leading inspirationally in various areas is ineffective. Conversely, a principal who is a good instructional leader, for instance, but who ignores managerial and administrative exigencies will ultimately fail, too.

Principals who manage their schools effectively consider these issues, among others:

- *School building opened in a timely and efficient manner*
- *Heating and air conditioning maintained*
- *PTA planning room designated*
- *Making sure fire safety regulations are adhered to*
- *Security officials in place for morning duty*
- *Substitute teachers called as needed*
- *Supplies for main office ordered*
- *Book requisitions secured*
- *Office and building decorated*
- *Ensuring custodians are doing their job*
- *Preparing and monitoring the budget*
- *Conferring with office staff and other administrative personnel*

- *Organizing a filing system*
- *Assigning personnel for various duties (e.g., bus, yard, and hall)*
- *Monitoring morning and afternoon lineups (outdoor and indoor)*

5. Research indicates that principals, especially new ones, retain their jobs because of their managerial role but would rather delegate management functions to others so that they could devote more time to instructional leadership.

Recent research confirms that this statement is indeed accurate (Oplatka, 2005). Managerial functions and duties are fundamental to your success as principal. Before you can effectively engage in instructional, collaborative, and transformational leadership you must demonstrate competence in managing school operations on a daily basis. Imagine a school beset by chaos due to inefficient and inappropriate scheduling of classes and teachers. Imagine a school that is unsafe because of poor or inadequate deployment of aides. Imagine teachers complaining that they have few, if any, supplies such as chalk, paper, and textbooks. According to Oplatka, "Management refers to all technical aspects of the principals' work associated with day-to-day planning, coordination, control, budgeting and operation of the school in support of the instructional programme and associated school goals." Also included are the "assignment of teachers, the supply of resources and the scheduling of classes" (p. 46). Oplatka affirms that such management responsibilities are essential for the "survival and success of newly-appointed principals." "After all, in this initial stage of their career, principals still have to prove their competency and managerial skills in the basic elements of school management" (p. 46). Oplatka continues by explaining that as principals move into their midcareer phase, however, expectations change, with more emphasis expected in leadership skills beyond the management of their schools. Despite Oplatka's findings, many school systems certainly expect you to function effectively from the get-go in both management and leadership functions. Effective principals, from my experience, are able, with more experience, to delegate some of their managerial responsibilities so that they can devote greater attention to instructional and other forms of leadership.

6. Rankings of duties

See if the rankings in Tables 1 and 2, corresponding to the actual duties of principals and APs, match your own. The data are drawn from a formal study I conducted some time ago (Glanz, 1994) as well as recent informal data I've collected.

Table 1   Actual Duties of Assistant Principals: Rankings and Percentages

Duties	Rank	%
Student discipline	1	94
Lunch duty	2	94
School scheduling (coverages*)	3	93
Ordering textbooks	4	91
Parental conferences	5	91
Assemblies	6	91
Administrative duties	7	91
Articulation**	8	90
Evaluation of teachers	9	83
Student attendance	10	71
Emergency arrangements	11	63
Instructional media services	12	54
Counseling pupils	13	46
School clubs, etc.	14	41
Assisting PTA	15	35
Formulating goals	16	32
Staff development (inservice)	17	27
Faculty meetings	18	24
Teacher training	19	24
Instructional leadership	20	23
Public relations	21	9
Curriculum development	22	7
Innovations and research	23	5
School budgeting	24	3
Teacher selection	25	1

Coverages refer to scheduling substitute teachers to cover for absent regular classroom teachers.

**Articulation* refers to the administrative and logistical duties required to prepare for graduation (e.g., preparing and sending cumulative record cards for graduating fifth graders to the middle school).

Table 2   Actual Duties of Principals: Rankings and Percentages

Duties	Rank	%
Formulating goals	1	92
Administrative duties	2	91
Parental conferences	3	90
School budgeting	4	87
Student discipline	5	87
Faculty meetings	6	85
Lunch duty	7	82
Emergency arrangements	8	80
School scheduling (coverages*)	9	77
Evaluation of teachers	10	77
Staff development (inservice)	11	72
Assisting PTA	12	70
Teacher training	13	64
Ordering textbooks	14	58
Public relations	15	51
Instructional leadership	16	40
Teacher selection	17	28
Assemblies	18	17
Articulation**	19	12
Student attendance	20	11
Instructional media services	21	6
Counseling pupils	22	5
School clubs, etc.	23	3
Curriculum development	24	2
Innovations and research	25	1

*Coverages refer to scheduling substitute teachers to cover for absent regular classroom teachers.

**Articulation refers to the administrative and logistical duties required to prepare for graduation (e.g., preparing and sending cumulative record cards for graduating fifth graders to the middle school).

> **Reflective Question**
>
> 1. Draw some conclusions from the data above. How do principals and APs differ in their actual duties? How do the data reflect your actual duties and those of your APs, if you have them?

Now, peruse Tables 3 and 4, which indicate how APs and principals rank their duties in terms of importance, that is, what they would like to be involved in if they had their wish.

Table 3   Assistant Principals' Rankings of Their Duties for Degree of Importance

Duties	Rank	%
Teacher training	1	93
Staff development (inservice)	2	92
Curriculum development	3	91
Evaluation of teachers	4	90
Instructional leadership	5	90
Formulating goals	6	86
Innovations and research	7	83
Parental conferences	8	82
Articulation	9	82
School scheduling (coverages)	10	81
Emergency arrangements	11	80
Assemblies	12	80
Administrative duties (paperwork)	13	76
Instructional media services	14	68
Counseling pupils	15	61
Faculty meetings	16	55
Ordering textbooks	17	51
School clubs, etc.	18	45

(Continued)

Table 3 (Continued)

Duties	Rank	%
Assisting PTA	19	39
Student attendance	20	34
Student discipline	21	31
Lunch duty	22	25
Public relations	23	21
School budgeting	24	11
Teacher selection	25	9

Table 4   Principals' Rankings of Their Duties for Degree of Importance

Duties	Rank	%
Formulating goals	1	98
Administrative duties (paperwork)	2	94
Emergency arrangements	3	94
Teacher selection	4	89
School budgeting	5	88
Teacher training	6	85
Staff development (inservice)	7	85
Curriculum development	8	81
Evaluation of teachers	9	80
Faculty meetings	10	76
Instructional leadership	11	71
Innovations and research	12	65
Parental conferences	13	63
Public relations	14	61
Assisting PTA	15	55

Duties	Rank	%
Articulation	16	50
School scheduling (coverages)	17	45
Student discipline	18	25
Lunch duty	19	25
Assemblies	20	20
Instructional media services	21	15
Counseling pupils	22	15
Ordering textbooks	23	10
School clubs, etc.	24	8
Student attendance	25	5

Reflective Questions

1. Draw some conclusions from the data above. How do principals and APs differ in what they consider most important? What surprises you about the data, if anything? How do the data reflect your wishes and those of your APs, if you have them?

2. What conclusions can you draw from the data about principals' interest in administrative or operational leadership? Compare these conclusions with information gleaned from APs.

See Resource B for a more detailed survey to assess your role as operational leader.

CHAPTER ONE

Introduction

"The role of the principal as manager is key in the daily organizing, functioning, and execution of numerous processes and tasks that permit a school to accomplish its goals as a learning community."

—Marsha Speck

I t's not very glamorous to talk about management or operational leadership these days. Such leadership is too often taken for granted, yet as we mentioned earlier, it's important, because it serves as the foundation for all other forms of school leadership (see Figure 1.1). A perusal of recent books demonstrates that operational leadership is often neglected or given scant attention. The Davies (2005) book titled *The Essentials of School Leadership,* although a wonderful text covering a variety of important forms of leadership, including strategic, transformative, ethical, constructivist, poetical, emotional, and sustainable, omits any mention of the operational or managerial responsibilities of school leaders.

This book on operational leadership represents an important aspect of a principal's work. Each book in the series addresses a specific, important role or function of a principal. Discussing each separately, however, is quite artificial and a bit contrived. In fact, all seven forms of leadership (instructional, cultural, ethical/spiritual, collaborative, operational, strategic, and school-community) form an undifferentiated whole. Still, we can glean much from a more in-depth analysis of each form of leadership. It is with such understanding that this book is framed. Operational leadership reflects

1

an educational paradigm based on the following assumptions or premises:

- You, as principal, play the most vital role in managing school operations. In fact, without your commitment and efforts, little will be accomplished regarding other forms of leadership without dutiful attention to this one.

- Your effectiveness as a principal is predicated on willingness and ability to engage in all forms of leadership. Although management of day-to-day operations in your school building is vital, do not let yourself become immersed in managerial imperatives to the exclusion of other important forms of leadership.

> "School principals have an extraordinary opportunity to improve public schools."
>
> —Roland S. Barth

- Principal operational leaders balance the requirements of the organization with individuals' needs. In fact, good leaders fit organizational structures to suit individual needs. After all, an organization is made up of individuals in order to serve individuals. Too many administrators lose sight of this reality.

- A principal must possess the knowledge and ability to promote the success of all students by managing the organization, operations, and resources in a way that promotes a safe, efficient, and effective learning environment.

- Getting organized, managing facilities, handling the budget, attending to human resource issues, and communicating effectively form the essence of good practice as an operational leader.

- Managing a school is an important yet burdensome task. Some of you may have an AP or two to assist in these matters. Yet many, if not most, of you may not. Still, this book is premised on the notion that your obligations to operational leadership are nonetheless essential. Creative principals will find ways to balance operational imperatives with other forms of leadership.

- Finally, you cannot function as an operational leader, or any leader for that matter, without managing your own welfare. Taking care of yourself so that you may care for others is often forgotten.

Reflective Questions

1. Consider leaders you have known. Assess their operational leadership skills. What stands out as particularly noteworthy? Unworthy?

2. Assess the degree to which your school is well managed. Do you prefer to engage in nonoperational matters? If so, who's "watching the ship"? What else might you need to learn in order to function as a good manager?

3. What operational leadership challenges do you face? Explain.

4. React to the assumptions listed above. Which make the most sense to you?

* * * * * * * * * * * * * * * *

This book and series are also aligned with standards established by the prominent Educational Leadership Constituent Council (ELCC). ELCC standards are commonly accepted by most educational organizations concerned with preparing high-quality educational leaders and as such are most authoritative (Wilmore, 2002). The ELCC, an arm of the National Council for the Accreditation of Teacher Education, developed six leadership standards used widely in principal preparation. These standards formed the basis for this book and series:

1.0: Candidates who complete the program are educational leaders who have the knowledge and ability to promote the success of all students by facilitating the development, articulation, implementation, and stewardship of a school or district vision of learning supported by the school community.

2.0: Candidates who complete the program are educational leaders who have the knowledge and ability to promote the success of all students by promoting a positive school culture, providing an effective instructional program, applying best practices to student learning, and designing comprehensive professional growth plans for staff.

*3.0: Candidates who complete the program are educational leaders who have the knowledge and ability to promote the success of all students by managing the organization, operations, and resources in a way that promotes a safe, efficient, and effective learning environment.

4.0: Candidates who complete the program are educational leaders who have the knowledge and ability to promote the success of all students by collaborating with families and other community members, responding to diverse community interests and needs, and mobilizing community resources.

5.0: Candidates who complete the program are educational leaders who have the knowledge and ability to promote the success of all students by acting with integrity, fairly, and in an ethical manner.

6.0: Candidates who complete the program are educational leaders who have the knowledge and ability to promote the success of all students by understanding, responding to, and influencing the larger political, social, economic, legal, and cultural context.

* This standard is addressed in this book.

Readers should also familiarize themselves with ISLLC and National Association of Elementary School Principals standards (see, e.g., http://www.ccsso.org/projects/Interstate_School_Leaders_Licensure_Consortium/ and http://www.boyercenter.org/basicschool/naesp. shtml).

* * * * * * * * * * * * * * *

In order to establish a framework for the chapters, Figure 1.1 illustrates the role of the principal attempting to facilitate and influence the critical elements of operational leadership. Effective principals pay careful attention to this mundane yet important responsibility. Principals work best as operational leaders when they manage their school smoothly and efficiently, creating a conducive

Figure 1.1   A Model of Operational Leadership That Promotes a Safe,
Efficient, and Effective Learning Environment

learning environment so that all the other good and necessary work
in the school gets done with excellence.

* * * * * * * * * * * * * * * *

Allow me to offer a word on chapter format and presentation
of information. Information in each of the six main chapters
is presented as concisely as possible to make for easy and quick

reference reading. Each chapter begins with boxed material called "What You Should Know About." The box will list and briefly explain the concepts covered in each chapter. Certainly, each chapter will not cover every bit of information there is to know about a given topic, as mentioned earlier. Each chapter culls, though, essential knowledge, skills, and dispositions necessary for a successful principal.

A brief word on chapter organization is in order to facilitate reading. Chapter 2 includes some best practices for getting organized, which is so foundational for all operational work in schools. The third chapter highlights practices for managing facilities. Establishing a warm, safe, and secure school environment is among the first steps you take as operational leader. The fourth chapter addresses budgetary issues, over which principals across the country today are assuming greater control than ever before. Human resources management takes up the fifth chapter. Managing others is essential in our work. Chapter 6 discusses the importance of effective communication, without which confusion and chaos reign supreme. The final chapter addresses your personal management. Taking care of yourself is too often taken for granted, as we alluded to earlier. Taken together, these six chapters provide you with information and strategies that promote an efficient and effective school environment. This book is not meant to be the definitive treatise on operational leadership, but rather to raise some relevant issues for your consideration. It is my hope that the ideas in this book will give you pause to think about your own role in management issues.

As a concluding activity to this Introduction, read the boxed material that contains nine quotations meant to inspire and, more important, to provoke critical thinking about your role as operational leader. Read each quotation, and ask yourself these questions:

- What does the author convey about management, directly or indirectly (in other words, what's the message in a nutshell)?
- Critique the quotation. Does the thought reflect your beliefs? Explain.
- What practical step(s) could you take to actualize the idea behind each quotation?

Some Key Quotations Related to Operational Leadership

"School leaders must first of all be skillful managers. . . . Whatever else a district may want from its leaders, managerial skill is essential; without it, no school leader will last long."

—Stuart C. Smith and Philip K. Piele

"The overlap between leadership and management is centered on how they both involve influencing a group of individuals in goal attainment."

—Peter G. Northouse

"Success is good management in action."

—William E. Holler

"Principals must continue to upgrade their effective management practices that keep students safe and public policies and funds appropriately addressed, even as they commit their primary energies to the issues of teaching and learning."

—William A. Owings and Leslie S. Kaplan

"With the additional stress of federal and state mandates, we need every effective tool we can find to help our school principals and classroom teachers meet the new challenges of the 21st century."

—Jim R. Watson

"Organizational life need not be an endless series of meetings run by *Robert's Rules of Order*. There can and should be excitement and energy there."

—Susan R. Komives, Nance Lucas, and Timothy R. McMahon

"Viewing schools as relationships linked together as circuits is useful in understanding the interconnectedness of human social organizations and how information flows through them."

—Randall B. Lindsey, Laraine M. Roberts, and Franklin CampbellJones

"'A manager is responsible for consistency of purpose and continuity to the organization. The manager is solely responsible to see that there is a future for the workers.' [It is our responsibility

(Continued)

(Continued)

> as a society to manage our schools so that almost all students get a high-quality education]."
>
> —William Glasser, quoting W. Edwards Deming
>
> "Every great manager I've ever interviewed has it. No matter what the situation, their first response is always to think about the individual concerned and how things can be arranged to help that individual experience success."
>
> —Marcus Buckingham

CASE STUDY AND REFLECTIVE QUESTIONS

Anita Valez is proud of her school. She's worked hard, as have her teachers and staff. As a first-year principal, she was awarded Principal of the Year by the Central Office for her ability to provide "uncommon leadership and meticulous attention to managing" the district's most challenging school. Located in the "rough" part of town, PS 999, according to its mission statement, is a "diverse collaborative school community committed to excellence and equity." The statement elaborates:

> *We aim to provide for a clean, safe and orderly environment. Our students will learn about self, community and the world. They will have the opportunity to be problem solvers, critical thinkers and effective communicators. We will encourage students to experiment, predict and take risks. We will cultivate parent participation in all aspects of school life. We will embrace challenges and obstacles and learn from them and grow. We will continue to strive to reach our goal of creating a school of lifelong learners. Our job as leaders is to provide for a conducive learning environment so that all students can achieve their personal best.*

The following school demographics can be found on their Web page:

Students in full-time special education (self-contained students): **8.8%**

Students in part-time special education (mainstreamed students receiving pull-out services mandated by their Individualized Educational Plans [IEPs]): **6.2%**

Students participating in free or reduced-price lunch program: **82%**

English-language learners (ELLs): **11.8%**

Student stability (the percentage of students who remained at the school during the school year): **88.3%**

Ethnicity: Asian, **2.5%***; black,* **71.7%***; Hispanic,* **19.5%***; white,* **6.3%**

Ms. Valez is an eager, intelligent, and well-trained principal entering her second year. The district has recently given all principals control over fiscal spending and budgetary matters. Unlike her more seasoned colleagues, she is comfortable dealing with budgetary matters, because budget in the past never was as fully under the purview of a principal. In fact, Ms. Valez is so well versed in budgetary issues that she is often asked to offer assistance to other principals. "Ms. Valez is very shrewd and talented in combining strategic planning with budgetary matters," explains the district's superintendent. At a half-day training session for district principals, Ms. Valez explains how she integrates planning and budget:

"We take our agreed-upon vision and mission and then conduct a thorough needs assessment. The needs assessment is the most critical aspect of school-based budgeting, and now, under the lens of No Child Left Behind (NCLB) oversight, schools must address the importance of disaggregated data (subgroup analysis of achievement over a three-year period). We develop annual goals and measurable objectives. We determine what methods and strategies we may employ to achieve our goals and objectives. We develop an action plan for implementation. Then, we chart a preliminary budget to support the action plan. Our School Leadership Team works collaboratively on all these phases.

"As you set out your strategic plan, it is of utmost importance to think of it as an application for funding. You are in effect requesting funds for basic educational services as well as for supplemental educational services (e.g., Title I and other federal funds). It is so important to create a budget that will help you attain your goals and achieve your objectives. Allocating the right amount of money for those projects *that will help you achieve your goals is necessary. You must thoroughly think through your entire educational plan. Ask yourself, What do I want to accomplish? And how much money will it take to do so? When you write your budget, be mindful of restrictions and allowable charges.*

"The budget process first begins with a needs assessment. We should prioritize our needs. Under mandated services, of course, we include the principal, APs, the classroom teacher, desks, chairs, and mandated curriculum materials. Supplementary services are our main thrust. Keep in mind that Title I is not a mandated service. Student services are my number-one priority. Professional development expenditures are also considered at this point.

"Now that I have identified my needs, I must determine the cost of meeting those needs. I consider personnel (annual positions, including salary and fringe benefits) as well as hourly or per-session positions. Purchased services are identified here, too, such as the hiring of educational consultants. Finally, supplies, equipment, and material purchases are identified at this point.

"Once I determine costs, I must identify an appropriate funding source. I know that mandated instructional programs (e.g., literacy or mathematics) are a tax levy obligation. Supplemental funding pays for nonmandated services. Examples of mandated services beyond personnel may include basic equipment (desks, chairs, mandated curriculum materials), IEP and ELL mandates, and so forth. Supplemental services may include, for example, outreach services for attendance, professional development, extended-day programs, and parent involvement initiatives.

"Note that there really are three tiers of services:

- Mandated services that are a tax levy obligation
- Reimbursable funding that offsets the cost-specific mandated services for specific populations (such as Pupils with Compensatory Educational Needs—Limited English Proficiency [LEP] for ELLs and the Individuals with Disabilities Education Act for special education [IDEA])
- Reimbursable funding, such as Title I, that is truly supplemental

"As you know, there are generally four fund sources that we can consider:

- Requirements for all students—usually instructional programs and resources are included—and tax levy monies
- Mandated services—such as IDEA and other state-mandated initiatives (varies state to state)

- *Supplemental targeted needs (Title I to increase achievement of students who have not met or who are at risk of not meeting academic standards; Title III involving ELL)*
- *Competitive grants*

"*It's important to stress that supplemental services are meant to strengthen or add to services that are tax levy mandated. Reimbursable funds are used for these supplemental services, but remember, they cannot be used to pay for mandated services.*

"*Above all else, it's important to explicitly state in your strategic plan how you will use all available funds to accomplish your objectives. A rationale must be provided. See example excerpts below.*"

PS 999 Program: English as a Second Language (ESL). Note that our state mandates two levels of service (i.e., number of minutes per week) to ELLs. This is dependent on whether the student is classified as beginner or intermediate. Title III is the funding for supplementary services for the ELLs and provides for supplementary instruction such as an extended school day, professional development, and parental involvement.

Number of LEP students served 2006–2007: 20

1. *Description of program (including brief description of program, number of classes per program, languages of program, instructional strategies, etc.)*

"*PS 999 provides instruction to ELLs through its freestanding ESL program in kindergarten through fifth grade. For the 2005–2006 school year, 20 students participated in this program. For the 2006–2007 school year, it is anticipated that approximately 20 students will participate in this program. Progress will be measured by the New York State English as a Second Language Achievement Test (NYSESLAT). We have an ESL teacher for three full days. The teacher sees five groups of children on each of these days. The ESL teacher pulls children out for the majority of her classes. She pushes in whenever possible. In the ESL program, the language of instruction is English 100% of the time. In order to develop the phonemic awareness of students who are ELLs, the teacher includes lessons in oral language development. The four skills of listening, speaking, reading, and writing are included in each lesson.*

"*Students are taught reading through the Balanced Literacy approach. The teacher provides leveled book choices that are appropriate and appealing to ELLs. The teacher uses ESL strategies such as extensive use of visuals; repetition to promote oral language development; and content area ESL instruction related to mathematics, social studies, and science. During the spring semester, students are offered an additional time in preparation for testing in fourth and fifth grades."*

2. Parent involvement

"The parent coordinator assigned to our school pays particular attention to parents of ELL students, especially newcomers to the English-language school system. The parent coordinator and other school staff members endeavor to create a welcoming atmosphere. Parent orientation meetings are held during the fall and periodically during the year as new children arrive. PS 999 prides itself on supporting the efforts of families to be partners in the children's education. Parents are encouraged to join ESL adult education classes. These classes are held at various locations during both the day and evening. Information on times and locations is provided to parents whenever possible. Orientation is held at the beginning of the new school year. At orientation, a video describing the program is provided in various languages. When possible, letters to parents are provided in the dominant languages of our area. These languages include Spanish, Russian, Arabic, Chinese, and Albanian."

3. Staff development

"Our administrators, teachers, teaching assistants, and parents will participate in ongoing staff development sessions with issues related to core curriculum and how LEP students gain access to the core curriculum. ELL instruction support specialists, teacher center staff, and school-based staff will conduct interactive sessions. Some tentative topics for staff development include:

- *Identification of ELLs—tentative date, September 20, 2006*
- *Strategies for the regular classroom teacher of ELLs—tentative date, October 18, 2006*
- *Planning lessons to include all students*
- *Balanced Literacy for ELL students*
- *Mathematics for ELL students*
- *ESL in the content areas*

"Other staff development dates to be announced.
"PS 999 also has a teacher center that is available to all teachers."

Ms. Valez finishes her presentation and fields questions from her colleagues. She speaks with the superintendent afterward. "Budgeting is so important to my effectiveness as principal. Without mindful attention to my school's budget, I cannot accomplish all that I want to for my children. Sure, it's tedious and somewhat time-consuming. But I prefer to use the money allocated to me in ways that meet my goal and objectives. I can be accountable that way and do so much more good for my school. I can carry out my vision. All good principals should not delegate budgetary matters to anyone. They should take courses and attend all budget-related meetings religiously. After a short while, they will become familiar with the terminology and have greater confidence in using the monies allocated in ways that meet their school's unique needs. Principals as operational leaders function optimally when they have budgetary control."

The information used in this case study came in part from materials distributed from the Regional Operations Centers of the New York City Department of Education. Visit their Web site (http://www.nycenet.edu/administration/organization+of+the+DOE/ROC/Budget/) for much more detailed information. This information is merely illustrative, because information, policies, programs, and so forth will vary greatly from state to state and district to district around the country.

Reflective Questions

1. Why is Ms. Valez so committed to operational leadership?

2. What makes her efforts so unique?

3. To what degree have you attended to budgetary matters as part of your strategic plan initiative?

4. What other activities would you have engaged in related to operational leadership?

5. How might you demonstrate your commitment to operational leadership?

6. In what ways can such efforts affect student learning and, ultimately, achievement?

7. What else would you need to know about the budget process?

As mentioned in the Introduction, the chapter that follows builds upon the preceding information by highlighting some "best practices" for helping you serve as an operational leader. These ideas are not meant to be exhaustive of the topic, but merely a means to encourage thinking related to managing your school.

CHAPTER TWO

Best Practices in Getting Organized

"When we discuss the operations of the school, we mean the daily activities necessary to keep the school operating smoothly and efficiently."

—Elaine L. Wilmore

"Because organizations are complex, surprising, deceptive, and ambiguous, they are formidably difficult to understand and manage."

—Lee G. Bolman and Terrence E. Deal

"Organize the work, establish procedures, and identify a clear focus for the work so that you can achieve your goals."

—Barbara L. Brick and Marilyn L. Grady

"Doing a good job in leadership without ruining yourself in the process may be difficult if you are too much of a perfectionist or too much of a procrastinator."

—Donald Schumacher

U ndoubtedly, developing and maintaining efficient organizational skills is necessary to serve as a good manager. Think about the managers you know who are well organized. They are probably prompt, always seem to be on top of things, know where all papers are filed, and may at times even appear compulsive as they go about their daily tasks. Let's see how Roberta Rodriguez goes about handling all of her tasks:

Today was a typical day for Ms. Roberta Rodriguez, principal of Boynton High School, located in an affluent suburb of Chicago. In addition to preparing the day's scheduling and arranging for substitute teachers, she is involved in the all-too-mundane activities associated with her position as principal in a large school of nearly 3,500 students. Today, Ms. Rodriguez:

- distributed newly obtained textbooks to the English Department;
- selected Mr. William Johnson to escort the school band to the district's Open House celebration;
- reviewed legal mandates regarding the ELL program;
- decided to call an emergency grade conference to familiarize teachers about the newly adopted core content curriculum standards;
- dictated three letters to her secretary;
- prepared her budget report to the superintendent;
- recommended to the School-Community Council that Ms. Sylvia Barnett be selected as Parent-of-the-Month;
- responded to 35 "urgent" e-mail messages;
- completed her evaluation report of the after-school student at-risk program;
- began a needs assessment in order to implement an interdisciplinary team teaching program;
- placed a new admission in Mr. Steve Goldman's already overcrowded home room;
- walked around school with custodian to inspect possible fire safety hazards;
- proofread revised school handbook;
- suggested that the art and science programs be revised;
- scheduled time for the Chess Club to meet during period 4;
- recommended suspension for Maurice and Christopher for pulling the fire alarm at dismissal;
- conducted a bus safety drill;

- updated standard operational procedures for class trips;
- monitored attendance and tardiness reports for the 12th grade;
- interviewed a prospective teacher for a vacancy in the English Department;
- supervised first-period lunch duty in the cafeteria;
- determined that Ms. Joan Smith, an untenured teacher, should not be rehired for the next semester;
- observed Ms. Phyllis Williams, a veteran teacher, during the fourth period;
- conducted a post conference with Ms. Williams during the eighth period.

As you can see, Ms. Rodriguez's day, like those of most other educational leaders, was not only arduous and frenetic, at times, but also filled with many situations that required good, if not superior, organizational skills. Quite often, we are challenged by these mundane and not-so-mundane activities related to student discipline, administration of school policies, evaluation of teachers, graduation activities, emergency arrangements, efficacy of new curricula, implementation and evaluation of varied school programs, and much more. Clearly, Ms. Rodriguez has it together, because she pulls off all her responsibilities with much aplomb.

In contrast, a disorganized leader might have great ideas about the many aspects of educational reform but doesn't possess the managerial skills necessary to pull them off. He may appear disheveled, with his desk in disarray, at a loss for what to do next, running aimlessly from one event or matter to another without a rhyme or reason; or he may even appear lazy or uninterested. One's personality and environmental influences play a role in determining the extent to which someone is organized. One can still learn, however, how to more efficiently go about organizing one's day with its varied activities and concomitant pressures. It's important for each of us to assess the degree to which we are organized. Some of us may feel we already are organized, but reality may present a different picture. Ask yourself these questions, among others that you can come up with on your own:

- Am I continually misplacing important papers?
- Why can't I seem to find that item on my desk or in my files?
- Do I rarely file important papers?

- Do I have a filing system I can rely on?
- Does my desk look like a tornado hit?
- Are my drawers so messy I'd be embarrassed to show anyone?
- Do I tend to forget appointments?
- Why do people say about my organizational skills?

Many self-help books have been published on the subject. Some of them do help. Ask a friend or colleague or two to assess your organizational skills. Don't be defensive. Listen, learn, and see if you can't apply some of the best practices in this chapter to assist you. I tested this suggestion on my administrative assistant. I called her into my office and asked her, "Sue, am I organized?" Although her response didn't surprise me, it did compel me to reflect and try to change. She said, "Organized? I know few others more so . . . ugh, but . . . you are so compulsively driven it drives some of us up the proverbial wall." She smiled and ended by saying, "We still love you." Surely I was aware of my compulsivity. I have to have my desk and office in order before I can begin to write, for example, even though the mild disarray has nothing to do with my writing. I have found that my mild tendency for OCD has helped me enormously to succeed and accomplish. Thankfully, it does not thwart my progress in any way, as may occur with severe forms of the disorder. Still, I said to myself, "Chill out, man"—as I really try to do. Conduct your own self-assessment, and include others' reactions. Take steps at honing and controlling your organizational skills. Doing so will help you become a more effective manager.

> "Effective leaders in today's world must be proficient at juggling."
>
> —Heidi Shaver

As noted in the Introduction, one of the major premises of this work is that your ability to organize your work environment is critical to your success as principal. No one wants a principal who has a reputation for being so disorganized that little gets accomplished in an efficient and expeditious manner. Well-organized principals are:

- on top of things in their school,
- prepared for upcoming meetings,
- able to prepare nearly flawless schedules,
- able to manage their time well,

- forward-thinking strategic planners,
- amiable and willing to assist others in any way possible,
- able to put into practice and exhibit many of the best practices that follow.

Reflective Questions

1. Have you conducted an assessment of your organizational skills? If so, what have you discovered?

2. What steps might you take to assist you in whatever direction you may need?

3. What suggestions might you make to a colleague who is much less organized than yourself? Is this person willing to listen and improve? Why or why not?

Regarding the last question, it's important to note that some people will refuse to acknowledge their deficiencies in this area. Either they will eventually fail, or they will find someone to assist them in some way. A successful principal I happen to know quite well has serious organizational skill problems. She's a visionary thinker; that's her greatest strength. But she realizes her deficiencies and appoints her administrative assistant to oversee all organizational matters. She has improved tremendously over the years, because she goes out of her way to try to find ways of getting more organized (e.g., by reading self-help books and trying to implement some of the best practices highlighted in this chapter), but deep down she's comfortable about the way she operates (she's very talented in many areas of management and leadership). Still, she understands the great advantage of being organized. She recently purchased a Palm Pilot, which she uses religiously. It has helped her enormously.

The boxed material on the next page summarizes the ideas highlighted in this chapter. The list is not exhaustive, but is merely meant to highlight some key concepts and ideas that successful operational leaders should know as they hone their organizational skills. Brief reflective activities follow each major concept to provoke thought on ways to implement or further understand each idea.

What You Should Know About Getting Organized

- **Eight Organizational Tips**—We discuss Simon and Newman's (2004) suggestions to enhance your organizational skills.
- **Preparing the Schedule**—We review some suggestions for learning how to schedule.
- **Managing Time**—This section provides specific suggestions from several authorities on getting the most out of time.

---

1. EIGHT ORGANIZATIONAL TIPS

Simon and Newman's (2004) work is representative of the recent efforts among researchers and practitioners to view both leadership and management as interrelated and necessary roles and duties of principals in the 21st century. They acknowledge the urgency of addressing our managerial responsibilities so that we may more effectively attend to leadership at its various levels. They clearly realize that a principal must display excellent management skills:

> Managing the day-to-day operation of a school is challenging, even on the best days. The principal has to juggle literally hundreds of issues, problems, and requests, from the mundane to the life threatening. By the end of a school day, a principal has fielded numerous phone calls and visits from staff, students, and parents and has made the many regular committee meetings, class visits, and activities that constitute school life. (p. 1)

Both authors have extensive experience as principals, and they outline "some time-tested methods that will help you keep the never-ending paperwork requirements under control and allow you to allocate time to attend to the most important activities of an effective leader" (p. 1). The following are just some of their suggested methods:

Method 1: Setting up Your Organizational System

It is likely that as a new principal you are entering a school that has established ways of processing information and handling administrative matters. These ways of dealing with management issues have probably been set up by your predecessor. Her or his secretary is probably the gatekeeper of these logistical operations. Your first task in setting up your own organizational approach is to understand what already is in place. Ask your secretary the following questions, among others:

1. Is there a system in place to manage matters in the main office?

2. Is there a filing system in place, and what is it?

3. How are problems, administrative as well as personnel issues, dealt with?

4. How is the schedule of the principal kept?

5. How are emergencies or calls for the attention of the principal prioritized?

6. What is the schedule of personnel working in the office?

7. How are incoming phone calls handled, and by whom?

8. Is there anything else I need to know about in order to manage this office and school?

Although some procedures for managing the office and school affairs are in place, too often you'll find that there's no systematic way of handling these administrative exigencies. "Well, anyone who's around handles the situation," responds one secretary to a new principal. "You have to learn how to think on your feet here. We all do our 'thing.'" As principal, you should develop a systematic method of organization that matches your preferred style of managing with the skills and capabilities of your administrative staff. Establish definite procedures for specific events and issues along with specific people responsible for different matters. For instance, parents who show up without an appointment and demand to see the principal should be greeted by Ms. Baldwin, administrative assistant to the principal. She has been trained in dealing calmly and professionally with a variety of parental issues. At that initial contact, after hearing the complaint or issue, she makes the decision of where and to whom the parent should be referred. In some cases it might be one of the APs, and in other cases it might be the principal. In Ms. Baldwin's absence, a back-up assistant and a chain of command, so to speak, are identified.

Other procedures for dealing with a plethora of issues and circumstances should be identified, reviewed, accepted by those involved, and written. A Procedures Manual for dealing with administrative matters should be developed and periodically reviewed and updated. Certainly, circumstances will present themselves that do not easily fit into a pre-specified category. Nevertheless, developing a systematic, not haphazard or fly-by-your-pants, approach will go a long way toward better management of your school.

> "Principals who are good managers must have strong organizational skills."
>
> —Marsha Speck

Method 2: Make To-Do Lists

Think through and develop a list of goals and objectives you need to accomplish. Develop a yearlong set of objectives as well as quarterly ones. Keep separate lists, either in hard copy or as a computer file. For instance, you will know in August that by October 15 you must submit an interim report to your superintendent. List that responsibility on your yearlong and quarterly to-do lists. Create a spreadsheet listing the duty and boxes for "accomplished," "in progress," "needs more research," and so forth. Referring to and updating these lists are necessary. Simon and Newman (2004) suggest that you save these lists, something I personally do not do, but it's a good idea. They explain, "Your saved to-do lists provide a record of how you allocate and use time. Over time," they continue, "the lists may become part of the evidence needed to support staffing and budget needs" (p. 3).

Method 3: Keep Up With Mail

Develop a system. Develop something you feel comfortable with. Some principals prefer to have their mail screened, opened, and filed by a trusted secretary. Others, like myself, prefer to open and deal with my own mail. Simon and Newman (2004) comment that e-mail "has become a blessing and a burden" (p. 4). For me, it is essential and the preferred way of communicating, other than communicating in person, of course. I like e-mail because it gives me a sense of control. I can hit "delete" or "send." I find it quick and easy.

I even enjoy receiving e-mail despite the myriads of junk mail we're subjected to on a daily basis. Some of my colleagues call me a masochist because of my preference and devotion to e-mail correspondence. Some cautions about use of e-mail are relevant here:

1. Know that everything and anything you write can be read by anyone, so don't write something that you don't want blasted over the loudspeaker. I learned this lesson the hard way.

2. Think before you hit the "send" button. E-mail cannot be retrieved once sent.

3. Reread your important e-mails looking for simple errors or gross misstatements. E-mail correspondences can be misinterpreted easily. A joke or offhanded e-mail statement can be interpreted as derogatory, whereas when communicating in person, you can monitor the message through voice inflections and body language. Misinterpretations are common. I have had occasion to apologize for an e-mail message that was interpreted one way when in reality I meant something else.

Three final recommendations offered by Simon and Newman (2004, p. 4) include:

1. Create a system to sort and prioritize your mail.

2. Use your mail to support and compliment staff.

3. Make the resolutions to letters of complaint a priority.

Method 4: Make Special Folders

"Keeping track of hundreds of student and staff issues that come your way each week is a challenge" (Simon & Newman, 2004, p. 4). Developing special folders that are filed neatly and regularly by yourself or your secretary is essential. The paper trail will be overwhelming without a folder system. Folders can be kept for short-, middle-, and long-range issues, such as phone calls, staff conference materials, and strategic plan initiatives, respectively. This suggestion sounds simplistic, but how often are we attentive to it? If

> *"Failure to anticipate and think through the little details can overwhelm, destroy, and bury a principal."*
>
> —Paul G. Young

after several weeks you find your desk piled up with paperwork you can no longer identify, you are in desperate need of a filing system. Make certain you date and categorize each important document correctly and consistently. Your work will become more efficient and effective in the long run.

Method 5: Clip, Post, and Save Those Articles

Keeping a special folder for the following special items will help you in many obvious ways:

1. Newspaper articles about your school or district or about general educational issues

2. Magazine and journal articles (e.g., on topics such as special education, project-based learning, portfolios, testing)

3. Memoranda from key personnel in and out of the school (keep a separate folder for memos from your superintendent)

Such information is handy when you may need to write an article, make a speech, organize a bulletin board, create supporting documentation for a variety of matters, and so on.

Method 6: Create Your Own Filing System

Although relying on your trusted assistant or secretary to file important documents is acceptable, you should create your own filing system for items you may need quickly or when she or he is not around. Simon and Newman (2004) recommend that you should "do your own filing," "devise a filing system that matches your style and needs," and "use care when deciding what to file and what to discard, since this is a powerful decision" (p. 7).

Method 7: Carry Your Desk With You

We spend little time in our offices, so when we're out in the field, so to speak, we should carry essential items with us.

Although Simon and Newman (2004) do not suggest Palm Pilots but rather suggest filling a three-ring binder with information, I think the use of technology can allow us to manage our organizational lives much more efficiently (see next method).

Method 8: Technology Can Set You Free

Use of the latest technologies, such as digital cameras, digital video recorders, and memory sticks, can help you manage and organize many facets of your work.

Reflective Questions

1. Which of the suggestions provide some assistance for you?

2. What alternate tips can you offer others?

---

2. PREPARING THE SCHEDULE

Developing a master schedule takes practice. Many management tasks are learned best on the job. During your supervisory internship, you likely were exposed to scheduling experiences. You may have read some accounts of scheduling, but we really learn best by doing, and sometimes by trial and error. Planning schedules is one of those areas that is best learned through practice. Some general guidelines, though, are in order:

- Practice using a mock schedule. Your school is K–5 with two classes per grade level. Twelve teachers in total each must be scheduled for lunch, a preparation period, and a period in which a cluster (art, music, or physical education) teacher takes the class (one period a day). For instance, the art teacher takes them on Mondays, the music teacher on Wednesdays, and the physical education teacher on Fridays. Considering an eight-period day (no block scheduling), develop a schedule. What other information might you need to know to proceed?

- Seek advice from an experienced AP. That's what I did when my principal asked me to develop the schoolwide schedule for the upcoming year.

- Gather all necessary information. Collect last year's schedule, teacher requests, room allocations, student lists, and so forth.

- Ask the principal for advice. Solicit input from the principal.

- Develop the schedule while away from school. In my case, the principal gave me two days off. In the quiet of my apartment, I was undisturbed and able to give full attention to this tedious assignment.

- Use 3 × 5 index cards, and lay them out on a large table. Record all information on a master sheet as you go along. At the end of the process, compare the information on index cards with the master sheet.

- Double- and triple-check everything. After the first draft is completed, review the schedule looking for conflicts and other problems. Invite a friend or colleague to look it over as well. Even ask a teacher in your school to preview the schedule before mass dissemination.

- Attend a workshop. Although I learned the hard way (by myself), I'd recommend that you attend a training session, either at a conference or at the district office. Perhaps a more experienced AP can tutor you as well.

Reflective Question

1. Why is learning how to schedule important as an operational leader; after all, can't you simply delegate the responsibility to someone else? What may be some advantages of doing it on your own?

---

3. MANAGING TIME

Which would you choose, a million dollars in cash, or a penny that would double in value every day for 30 days? On first impulse, the average person would choose the million dollars. The far wiser choice, however, is the penny that would double itself daily. Although on day 6 you will have only 32 cents, by day 28 you will have accumulated $1,342,177. On day 29, you will have more than $2.6 million.

This demonstrates the compound interest power of positive small steps. The snowball effect, over time, becomes immensely fruitful.

> *"Time management is really a misnomer—the challenge is not to manage time, but to manage ourselves."*
>
> —Stephen R. Covey

Reflective Question

1. How does this "sage" advice help you in terms of approaching managing time as principal?

What did George Washington, Martin Luther King Jr., and Albert Einstein have in common? They, like you, lived. They all had 24 hours in a day. They accomplished much in their lifetime. Others had the same amount of time but were not able to accomplish as much. Now, I don't really know what led to their success, but successful people do use their time wisely. How might you use your time most efficiently and effectively in order to engage in those seemingly unending tasks?

I am certain that you could spend 24 hours a day every day for a month at work and still not feel that you've scratched the surface to accomplish all the work that must be done. We all have felt that way. However, these feelings can sometimes paralyze us into doing less work, because we rationalize, "Well, I'll never be able to finish all this work." Such thinking is dangerous and self-limiting. By following these few suggestions, you might be able to accomplish more than you thought possible. These suggestions and activities are part of the arsenal of every good school manager.

1. *Set a timetable.* If you have a project or report for yourself that seems overwhelming at first, set a realistic timetable for yourself. When will you complete the first draft? So, at the outset of the semester, you should set a date when you want to "see" the first draft, say, October 15. Break up the major components of the report and establish preset dates for yourself.

2. *Reward yourself.* Using some behavior management theory, tell yourself (for some, actually writing it down on your calendar may be more powerful) that after the project is completed and submitted, you will visit the local ice cream store for your favorite treat. Setting several rewards like this throughout the year might just give you some extra pounds, but some of my students say it also "does the trick." "I never missed one deadline . . . and it was lots of fun anticipating my reward."

3. *Learn to say no.* Brock and Grady (2004) state:

> No principal can do everything and do it well. When asked to do something, consider priorities. Say "yes" to the things that match goals. For other opportunities that do not match goals, be gracious, but firm: "No, I'm over-committed right now, but thank you for the offer." (p. 75)

4. *Set aside a time of day to work.* Trying to fit in work on that project throughout the day may be difficult and stressful. Select one particular time of day to work. It's the time you know you'll devote to thinking or writing. For some of you, the best time might be 7:00 a.m. so you can have 60 minutes of uninterrupted work before others arrive. For night owls, it might be 11 p.m. Some principals I know say that they go to bed at 9:30 p.m. or so after an exhausting day, sleep for 6 hours, awaken at 3:30 a.m., work for two "wonderfully productive hours," and then catch a nap for an hour or two. One reported, "After trying this twice, I was hooked. It works great for me. Not every day certainly, but twice a week. I find that the three or four hours spent this way is equivalent to 15 hours spread out otherwise in which I'm harried and inattentive."

Simon and Newman (2004) address the perceived time constraints we have as principals: "There is never enough time to do it all and to do it right" (p. 17), or so it seems. Effective managers are aware of time constraints, yet they seem to accomplish a great deal, because they allocate their time wisely and efficiently. All of us have 24 hours a day, so why is it that some people waste away their time with inane matters, yet others seem to accomplish so much? It's a matter of perspective, I believe. It's also a matter of how one approaches one's tasks. Let's say you have a 20-page report due at the end of the month. If you procrastinate and wait until the last weekend before it's due, you'll likely come up with an inferior product, at best. If you wait to find a few hours to work, those precious hours may be fleeting or may never arrive, given our hectic schedules. However, if you discipline yourself to write a few paragraphs a day over the course of the month, you'll more than likely complete the project with enough time for proofreading and fine-tuning. In the end, though, whatever approach you use, it should match your working style and preference, as long as the end product is good. You may feel comfortable with an approach, but if the approach yields inferior work, then you'll have to come up with an alternate strategy.

Here are some of Simon and Newman's (2004) "practical tips on how principals can organize and use their time wisely" (p. 17):

Method 1: Building Your Calendar

Simon and Newman (2004) recommend that you keep your own calendar. Electronic calendars are highly recommended, unless you insist on a paper one. Electronic calendars are very easy to use and can be updated by your secretary and made available for others to view. But managing your own calendar is strongly suggested. That way, you can make the most of your own appointments and schedule enough time in between. Instruct your secretary with specific guidelines should you decide to have her or him make most of your bookings. Always set aside reflection time in your day. In other words, block out 30 to 45 minutes daily in which you can spend time alone reflecting on various projects, events, or other matters. Instruct your staff to interrupt you only in an emergency. You can use this time to rejuvenate, because when you are refreshed you will be able to accomplish much more in a given time.

Method 2: Being in Two Places at Once

You are usually invited to simultaneous events. How can you attend both? First of all, careful and prompt recording of appointments on your calendar is a must. Second, although you may not be able to attend each event fully, do everything you can to at least show up; make your presence known; and excuse yourself, explaining that you must attend another event. Try to avoid such conflicts by "people-calendaring," so that you don't get a negative reputation regarding never staying for very long at an event.

Method 3: Meetings

Meetings are part of our existence in organizational life. Following several guidelines is crucial to making time for these many meetings:

Limit the meetings you call or attend. Only call or attend meetings that have a specific purpose or intended outcome. Carefully plan all agendas, and keep to a strict timetable. Invite all significant parties, and don't conduct meetings without their attendance. If you do, then you might have to call another repeat meeting in the future. Simon and Newman (2004) conclude, "Meetings should and can be a place to build camaraderie and support for your school's culture and vision" (p. 20).

Method 4: Getting Started

Getting organized is a key to managerial success. "The best way to get started each morning is to prepare for it the day before," explain Simon and Newman (2004). They continue, "Taking ten minutes before you leave at the end of the day to preview the schedule for the coming day goes far in making your mornings go smoothly" (p. 21).

Method 5: Coffee Shop Time

In a previous suggestion I advised you to close your door and schedule some reflective time. Simon and Newman (2004) believe that such isolated time is unrealistic given how hectic things can get in a school. You're unlikely, they say, to have quiet time for very long before an "emergency" arises. They suggest, rather, getting out of the school. Perhaps visit a local library or even a coffee shop. They relate: "One busy principal makes his neighborhood coffee shop his afternoon stop. In an hour over a cup of coffee, he dispenses with the mail, writes memos, and organizes materials for the coming day." This activity has further advantages: "The stop also serves as a transition from work to home, enabling him to arrive home ready to give full attention to family responsibilities and needs" (p. 22).

Simon and Newman (2004) make numerous other suggestions throughout their excellent book, which, by the way, is listed later in this book as a Best Resource in Resource C. For example, they explain that telephone interruptions are very common and can take time away from other important matters. Knowing how to use the phone is critical to your success. The authors recommend that you return calls as soon as you can. Doing so can avert potential problems. Devote a specific time of day to returning calls. Having your calls screened by your secretary saves a great deal of time.

Reflective Questions

1. How might these suggestions assist you with managing your time?

2. How does managing time well help get you better organized?

CONCLUSION

Every principal knows how important good organizational skills are to his or her work. In this chapter, we've discussed some suggestions for getting organized. We've indicated that scheduling is necessary to keep everyone in the school on task and organized. Finally, principals who are organized usually manage their time well.

The essential message here is that operational leadership in all its facets necessitates that you possess adequate skills of organization. Assess your ability to organize, and take appropriate steps to improve in this area.

CHAPTER THREE

Best Practices in Managing Facilities

"The principal has a key role in the planning and operation of the school facility."

—Thelbert L. Drake and William H. Roe

"From the earliest research to the present day, the principal's establishment and maintenance of a safe, orderly school environment has been identified as the most fundamental element of effectiveness."

—Kathleen Cotton

"Handling the business affairs of a school well provides a credibility to internal and external publics so that other less visible or measurable results can be achieved."

—Thelbert L. Drake and William H. Roe

DeRoche (1987) explains the relationship between the effectiveness of managing school plant and facilities and student learning in your school building. He says, "The physical aspects of the school plant and maintenance of its facilities contributes to or detracts from a school environment—its culture and its climate" (p. 281). As principal, you are charged with the responsibility of inspecting, managing, evaluating, and improving your plant and its facilities. You need to attend to five major responsibilities, according to DeRoche:

> the efficient and effective use of the building itself, the operation and care of the building and grounds, the proper management of school supplies and equipment, the safety and security of the plant and facilities, and the evaluation of personnel responsible for its care and upkeep. (p. 281)

DeRoche (1987, pp. 281–282) highlights and reviews the following principles and practices related to effective management of plant and facilities:

1. Theoretically, the school plant and its facilities should be influenced by the education programs and school services. In practice (though in many instances this is not the case), the school plant sometimes influences the school programs. The principal and others should be aware of the extent to which this exists.

2. Plans should be developed to use all of the space within the school. Space should not be wasted.

3. The school plant and its facilities should be modified to meet the needs and changes required by the educational program or school services (including special education students).

4. Safety, security, comfort, and adaptability should be essential factors in plant and facilities management.

5. The proper care of school plant and facilities requires the involvement of faculty, staff, and students.

6. Plans should be developed for the proper supervision and management of the plant and its facilities, supplies, and equipment.

7. Wherever possible, the principal should delegate responsibility for plant management to an AP or a custodian.

8. The principal should continuously evaluate educational needs and services and determine the extent to which the physical facilities, supplies, and equipment are meeting these needs.

9. School grounds and its equipment should reflect educational, recreational, and community needs.

10. Purchasing of school supplies and equipment should, wherever possible, be centralized and result from bids.

Consider the following set of questions as we analyze DeRoche's (1987) description of the major responsibilities of a principal related to facilities management:

Efficient and effective use of the building itself:

1. Do you solicit input from teachers and staff about use of space in the building?

2. Is space utilization in your building efficient?

3. Do you consider use of building during after-school hours?

4. Do you have some sort of chart or spreadsheet that can be used to check and monitor use of space in the building?

5. Can you tell at any time of day what rooms are not being used?

6. Is it possible you might have surplus school space that could be rented out to community groups in order to bring in revenue for the school?

7. Does the school board or central office have policies and procedures in place for community use of the school?

Operation and care of the building and grounds:

1. Did you know that you—not the custodian—are responsible for proper maintenance of the school plant and facilities, internal and external?

2. Do you have a plan for inspecting the plant and its facilities?

3. Do you have a good relationship with custodial services, and do you meet with the chief custodian regularly?

4. How do you assess care and maintenance of the school and its facilities?

5. When you walk around the building, do you have a chart or some sort of checklist to monitor facilities including plumbing, electrical systems, safety devices, heating/air conditioning systems, corridors, hallways, and so on?

6. Do you inspect the exterior of the school on a regular basis?

7. What do you look for on these inspections?

8. What would you do if you suspected that asbestos was somewhere in the building?

9. With whom would you consult about major and minor repairs in the building?

10. How do you conserve energy in the building?

11. Have you formed a committee to discuss school care and maintenance issues?

12. Do you document everything when it comes to maintenance and care of the school plant and its facilities?

13. Who oversees your role as principal in regard to these issues?

Proper management of school supplies and equipment:

1. What process have you established to requisition for supply and equipment needs in your school?

2. Who determines whether or not an item will be purchased?

3. Who's in charge of the entire process?

4. What procedures do you have for purchasing these items?

5. How do you monitor goods received from these purchases?

6. What mechanisms have you established to prevent damage or theft of supplies and equipment?

7. Do you have adequate storage place for these items?

8. Is storage of these items efficient, neat, and orderly?

9. Who's in charge of overseeing storage and distribution to faculty and staff?

10. Have you established some sort of evaluation form to assess how supplies and equipment are managed in your school?

11. Are all your procedures for management of supplies and equipment standardized?

12. Are they written and codified?

13. If someone asked you for an inventory of all instructional materials in your school, would you have one readily available?

14. Have you designated a committee to oversee these operations?

15. What is the extent of your involvement in all of the above?

Safety and security of the plant and facilities:

1. To what extent and in what ways have you made your faculty and staff aware of safety and security issues?

2. Have you involved students, parents, and other community members?

3. Do you have a written and standardized set of procedures for emergencies that might arise?

4. Is there an Emergency Team committee in place?

5. Are rules and regulations known by all?

6. Have you provided inservice training on safety and security issues to all employees?

7. What steps have you taken to ensure safety and security in transportation-related areas?

8. What steps have you taken to ensure safety and security in the cafeteria?

9. How do you draw attention to the need for the importance of these issues?

10. Are you in contact with the fire department regularly?

11. What about the police department?

12. Do you know the names of key personnel to contact in both the fire and police departments?

13. Have they visited the school within the last year?

14. Are fire drill and evacuation procedures known to all and practiced regularly?

15. Have you conducted, for instance, a mock terror alert?

16. Is safety part of the student curriculum?

17. How many assembly programs have you conducted on these topics over the past two years?

18. Do you have consistent and efficient procedures to document all accidents in your building?

Evaluation of personnel responsible for its care and upkeep:

Evaluation of custodial staff is critical here. Information about custodians can be found later in this chapter.

This chapter will highlight varied ways you as the principal can apply some of DeRoche's (1987) principles of facilities management.

What You Should Know About Managing Facilities

- **Coordinating Safety and Security**—Marzano's (2003) five action steps for an orderly school environment are discussed, as are other primary aspects of safety and security.
- **Overseeing the Cafeteria**—This section provides an outline of ideas related to many aspects of cafeteria management.
- **Working With the Custodian**—We discuss selected suggestions for working well with the custodian.
- **Conducting a Facilities Evaluation**—This section provides a checklist to consider when conducting such an evaluation.

---

1. COORDINATING SAFETY AND SECURITY

Researchers and practitioners alike understand the importance of establishing a safe and orderly school environment in order to lay the groundwork for academic achievement. We are all very much

> "It falls to the principal to get things right."
>
> —Sally J. Zepeda

aware of the rising incidence of violence in schools. Parents are rightly concerned about their children's safety. Principals are held accountable, more so than ever before, to ensure a safe, violence-free school building. Marzano (2003) recommends five action steps to achieve such a safe environment. Your role as principal is critical in establishing such a milieu in your school:

• Action Step 1: "Establish rules and procedures for behavioral problems that might be caused by the school's physical characteristics or the school's routines" (Marzano, 2003, p. 55). Quite often, the physical characteristics of a school building might create a potentially negative school environment (e.g., narrow hallways, poorly lit restrooms, blind alleyways). Principals should certainly identify potential trouble spots and take all feasible actions to correct a situation (e.g., checking lighting periodically, placing guards at critical spots at peak times). Marzano calls these actions principals need to take "ecological interventions." To implement them, he says, "a school must examine its physical structure and routines with an eye to heading off possible problems" (p. 55). Marzano (p. 55), citing the work of Nelson et al. (1998), makes six recommendations:

  • Reduce crowd density by utilizing all entrances and exits that are available.
  • Keep wait time to enter and exit common areas to a minimum.
  • Decrease travel time and distances between activities and events.
  • Use signs marking transitions from less controlled to more controlled space.
  • Use signs indicating behavioral expectations for common areas.
  • Sequence events in common areas to decrease the potential of overcrowding.

• Action Step 2: "Establish clear school-wide rules and procedures for general behavior" (Marzano, 2003, p. 55). Teachers have their classroom rules and procedures. Effective classroom managers connect class rules to schoolwide rules, ensuring no contradictions. Principals should discuss such coordination of rules and procedures at the classroom and schoolwide levels. Conduct assembly programs periodically to reinforce adherence to schoolwide behavioral policies.

• Action Step 3: "Establish and enforce appropriate consequences for violations of rules and procedures" (Marzano, 2003, p. 56). Principals, as teachers, should acquaint students in advance with the consequences of breaking schoolwide rules and procedures. Any consequences for violation of rules and procedures "must be fair and consistently administered" (p. 56). Marzano reviews a few common consequences employed by administrators. They include "verbal reprimands, disciplinary notices to parents, conferencing, after-school detention, out-of-school suspension, and expulsion" (p. 56).

• Action Step 4: "Establish a program that teaches self-discipline and responsibility to students" (Marzano, 2003, p. 57). Effective principals take proactive steps to prevent disciplinary problems (see discussion in Chapter 4).

• Action Step 5: "Establish a system that allows for the early detection of students who have high potential for violence and extreme behaviors" (Marzano, 2003, p. 57). Identifying trouble spots and students who are likely to cause disruptions well in advance can go a long way to preventing serious incidents.

Marzano (2003) concludes his discussion by explaining that addressing safety and order within a school is a "necessary but not sufficient condition for academic achievement" (p. 59). Still, he underscores the importance of his action steps for our work as operational leaders.

Although the principal is chiefly responsible and accountable for the safety of all school personnel and students, an AP may be assigned responsibility for school security and safety. The following outline is drawn from Glanz (2004) and the work of Dr. Thomas Montero and others who trained me back in the late 1970s and early 1980s, when I was studying for certification as a principal.

A. Responsibility for Matters of Safety
1. Ensure compliance with rules and regulations for maintenance of public order on school property. How do you assess compliance?
2. Supervise safety personnel under your jurisdiction. Do you delegate this responsibility? Explain.
3. Implement school safety plan. Is such a plan written, disseminated, and used? How often is the plan revised? How have 9/11 and incidents like Columbine affected your plans?
4. Update the school safety plan yearly to reflect changing problems and conditions in the school. Who's involved in the revision process?
5. Establish rules and procedures for visitors. How do you assess the effectiveness of these rules and procedures?

Establish a committee to develop a school safety plan. Ensure that everyone's responsibilities are clear. Meet often at the start, then regularly throughout the year, even when no incidents occur. Be proactive, not reactive. Anticipate problems and develop contingency plans.

B. School Security and Safety
1. Supervise school guards. How often do they receive a formal evaluation? Have you ever recommended that a guard be transferred? Explain.
2. Contact community and city agencies. Which agencies have you contacted during the past academic year?
3. Organize and operate fire and shelter drills. How do you assess such operations?
4. Coordinate with police department. When was the last time you did so?

You may not be able to do all this yourself. Encourage support and assistance from committee members and even parent volunteers.

C. Creation of Desirable School Climate
1. Develop, disseminate, and analyze results of a school-wide school climate survey.
2. Utilize results to improve relationships between students and administration, faculty and parents, parents and administration, and so forth.

3. Involve parents, students, school personnel, and community in formulation of school policies.

Developing an action research study here is a good idea. Utilize the school leadership team or whatever committee is at your disposal to administer a school climate survey. Committee members can gather, analyze, and interpret data. As committee chair, you should be integrally involved every step of the way. Use survey results to improve the security plan. Disseminate results and invite responses from the school community.

D. Preparation for Emergencies
   1. Help plan and implement a school safety/emergency plan.
   2. Coordinate with custodial staff on safety regulations, including checking of all fire extinguishers.
   3. Develop plan for false alarms.
   4. Have written instruction for all drills, including floor marshals, coverage of posts, and so on.
   5. Clarify procedures to be followed in case of accidents (emergency contact cards completed for all personnel and students, police contact, parent notification, etc.).
   6. Be sure that first aid instructions are posted and staff is trained in CPR: Contract with school nurse or local hospital officials.

Emergencies will occur. Anticipate the varied types of emergencies, and develop appropriate measures to deal with them. Constantly review procedures.

E. Special Rooms
   1. Shops: Attend to the following: signs on walls, written instructions to pupils, safety tests of all equipment, alertness to hazardous conditions, licensed teachers only, regulations for safety posted on walls, and so on.
   2. Gymnasiums: Check room, ensure equipment is properly spaced, check storage of equipment, and so forth.
   3. Science rooms, laboratories, storage rooms: Check condition of equipment, storage of flammable materials, licensed teacher for demonstrations of potential hazards, and so on.

Once a week, take a walk around the school with key committee members to look for potential "hot spots." Check room conditions, looking for cracked ceilings, leaky pipes, and so on. Check grounds and surrounding neighborhood as well.

F. Flow of Traffic
   1. Clearly labeled staircases—Describe your labels.
   2. Special directions—List your directions.
   3. Special instructions for elevator use—List your instructions.
   4. Hall coverage—Describe your coverage plan.
   5. Routines for walking in halls—List rules.
   6. Security assigned and on duty—Describe assignments.
   7. Routine for use of school buses (deployment of personnel to avoid accidents from oncoming traffic and from bus movements)—Describe routines.
   8. Arrival and dismissal procedures—Describe procedures and responsibilities in detail.
   9. Review procedures with committee members every month—Solicit input and recommendations for improvement.

G. Additional Student Regulations
   1. Constant supervision
   2. No students leave building without permission
   3. Window safety in classroom and hallways

> "In many school districts, concerns about violence have even surpassed academic achievement."
>
> —Pedro Noguera

Conduct assemblies to review security issues with students. Involve students on security committees.

H. Protection Against Intruders or Violence
   1. No person admitted unless on legitimate business
   2. All school personnel and students with appropriate, visible IDs
   3. Instructions to staff when suspected intruder is seen
   4. Deployment of security force to provide for maximum security at all times

5. Available list of emergency numbers—precinct, fire marshal, patrol officers, and so on
6. Police contacted quickly in case of emergency
7. Firm and swift action against intruders
8. Precinct notified when dismissal times are changed and when evening meetings and after-school events are scheduled

Conduct role plays to deal with intruders. Hold debriefing sessions with committee members. Review what went well and what may need improvement. Again, proactivity is key.

   I. Money and Other Valuables
1. Money to bank daily
2. School safe to house valuables and cash
3. Oversee school funds
4. Control of all keys and master keys
5. Instructions for staff regarding storage of personal valuables
6. Locker safety
7. Student orientation regarding bringing money, valuables, and other personal property to school

Disseminate to school staff procedures regarding valuables. Disseminate information verbally and in written memo form. Parents should also receive relevant information.

Reflective Question

1. To what extent are the aforementioned ideas feasible in your school? Explain in detail.

---

2. OVERSEEING THE CAFETERIA

In managing the school cafeteria, the roles of principal and AP (see Glanz, 2004) are essential in the following ways:

A. Participant in Formulating Policy
   1. Grade levels and number of students to be programmed for lunch periods
   2. Cafeteria environment: size, location, resources
   3. Routines: entrance, seating, serving, dismissal
   4. Staffing: personnel on duty
   5. Passes to bathroom, library, and other places
   6. Indoor versus outdoor lunch
   7. "Captive lunch" or leaving building (eating outside or going home)
   8. After-lunch activities: music, games, socializing, sports

When developing policies for cafeteria procedures, be sure to include others including teachers, cafeteria staff, and other school administrators. Brief others on your plan, asking for feedback and suggestions.

B. Problems Involved in Cafeteria Supervision
   1. Developing a plan for cafeteria duty: problem solving, proactive strategies, personnel, resources, emergency plan
   2. Disturbances (individual or group) or riots: plan of action
   3. Dealing with intruders, cutters, and so on
   4. Student dissatisfaction with cafeteria conditions (e.g., prices, menus and food preparation, waiting in line)
   5. Cafeteria traffic, passes, dismissal and entrance routines, and so forth
   6. Crowd control
   7. Conflict between students in cafeteria, between students and cafeteria personnel or school staff members
   8. Conflict between cafeteria personnel and custodial personnel on clean-up duties

Periodically, you should meet with your cafeteria committee to review problems that have arisen. What measures could be taken to minimize future incidents? What other measures can be taken to deal with similar problems in the future?

C. Assistant Principal's Responsibilities
   1. Teacher personnel
      a. Selection, training, and supervision of coordinators
      b. Training and supervision of assigned personnel

    c. Rotation of personnel

    d. Assignment of posts

    e. Clarification of duties

    f. Training in control of students

2. Interface with all personnel, including custodians, cafeteria personnel, school aides, security aides, dietician, and so on

3. Students

    a. Control and discipline

    b. Service squad composed of outstanding students

    c. Student cafeteria committee (to make recommendations for improvement)

    d. Drug problems

    e. Lavatories: supervision, passes, controls

    f. Need for constructive educational activities

4. Community complaints and requests; parent involvement and cooperation

Cafeteria duty is certainly not one of the more pleasant chores of principals and APs. However, running a smooth, efficient, and effective lunch program is essential. Poorly run lunch periods can endanger the safety of students and others and can have a deleterious effect on the rest of the school day. If chaos, for instance, reigns supreme during lunch time, carryover will occur in the classrooms after lunch. Use the general guidelines above (generated from Glanz, 2004 and the work of Dr. Montero and others who trained me for principalship) to develop a plan that fits your needs. Review your plan with your committee, and then monitor the plan carefully as you begin the implementation stage. I also suggest you visit some other schools that have efficient cafeteria operations to cull some ideas for your own school.

Reflective Questions

1. To what extent are you involved in overseeing the cafeteria? Explain.

2. What steps can you take if you do not have an AP to help you?

3. WORKING WITH THE CUSTODIAN

Many principals around the country have responsibilities to super-vise, administer, and evaluate custodial services in the school building. Here are some guidelines to follow:

- Consult with the district office regarding job descriptions, special arrangements, contractual agreements, or anything you may need to know about custodial services in your school.

- Get to know the custodian well. Conduct a background check by looking into references and past employment records. You don't have to undertake an extensive investigation, just enough to obtain sufficient information. You don't want surprises down the road.

- Get along with the custodian. Cooperate and meet regu-larly with the custodian. Positively reinforce his or her good work and service to the school. Develop good relationships with all the custodian's staff.

- Assist the custodian with any office work needed (e.g., schedules, personnel, budget).

- Schedule regular weekly meetings with custodian, always keeping him or her abreast of upcoming events, special projects, and so on.

- Walk the school and its exterior with the custodian at least twice a month.

- Mediate conflicts, if any, between teachers and custodial staff.

- Review custodial equipment needs.

- Develop concrete and measurable goals for the custodian.

- Develop a systematic and fair way to evaluate custodial work in the school. Adhere to district policies, if any, in this regard.

- Share evaluative findings with custodian in person and in writing.

Keep in mind these ideas:

A. Relationship With Custodians
  1. Fast channel of communication. What mechanisms do you have in place to expedite communication?
  2. Prompt service if hazards are noticed. How do you assess prompt service? What do you do if service is not prompt?
  3. Repairs where necessary. Are repairs completed in an efficient, prompt manner? How do you assess effectiveness of these repairs?
  4. Established precautions for inclement weather (snow removal, rubber mats for entrance, etc.). Do you have written regulations, and are they disseminated and available? Are they referred to and used? How do you know?

Develop positive relationships with custodial staff. Include them on important committees, soliciting their input. Their perspective is unique and invaluable. They'll appreciate your attentiveness and willingness to include them in these important matters.

B. School Plant
  1. Monitoring entrances
  2. Separate late door and personnel post
  3. Empty rooms locked
  4. Special locks for rooms with machines or equipment
  5. Special doors for computer labs and others
  6. Keys

Again, conduct walk-arounds, checking indoors and outside at least every week or even more often if needed.

Reflective Question

1. To what extent are you involved in overseeing custodial staff, and are you successful? Explain.

4. CONDUCTING A FACILITIES EVALUATION

Drake and Roe (2003) underscore the important role you play in facilities management. Whatever we are engaged in requires an evaluation in order to assess various outcomes. Although we often receive informal feedback from students, staff, and community visitors about school facilities, we need to undertake more formal evaluations. Principals who engage in best practice may compose questionnaires that address these areas of concern, among others:

- Physical structure of various facilities (e.g., computer lab or restrooms)
- Health standards in building (e.g., heating system, ventilation, cafeteria)
- Safety standards posted and known by all
- Communication equipment condition
- Aesthetic appearance of building
- Efficient use of energy

More specific items, according to Drake and Roe (2003), might include:

- Space accommodations for instructional purposes
- Access for students with disabilities
- Technologies available (e.g., wireless capability)
- Nonfunctional areas or dead spaces in building and safety concerns
- Ecological set-up of rooms and offices to best facilitate effective communication
- Storage facilities
- Electrical and plumbing facilities
- Planning of new facilities

Drake and Roe (2003) make the connection between facilities management and education when they state that "in the evaluation of the facility, the principal will be focusing on the relationship between the building and the educational programs that building is to serve." They continue, "Once the process of establishing priorities is completed and the staff to be involved in the evaluation understand the process as it applies to them, the mechanics of the evaluation (i.e., completing the forms or surveys, . . .) can be carried out efficiently" (p. 475). They conclude by making the connection between facilities and student achievement clear: "A key thought is that the term *facility* implies just that—the building should facilitate positive learning. The principal's challenge is, in the face of rapid changes, to seize quickly expanding opportunities to keep the building as a facilitating tool" (p. 486).

Reflective Questions

1. What other aspects would you include in a facilities evaluation?

2. What else would you do to ensure that the facilities "facilitate" learning schoolwide? Explain in detail.

CONCLUSION

Few, if any of us, will ever receive a standing ovation or an accolade of any sort for our diligent and competent attention to facilities management. Still, we know how important this work is to facilitate a conducive learning environment for all students in our school. If Abraham Maslow (1954) taught us, as he did, that security is a prerequisite to higher-order needs such as self-fulfillment, then certainly a similar analogy can be proffered here. By carefully planning and maintaining school operations, including facilities, we are providing a necessary and strong foundation for student learning in our schools.

CHAPTER FOUR

Best Practice in School Finance and Handling the Budget

"To manage the organizational and operational facets of the school effectively, it is essential to have appropriate resources."

—Elaine L. Wilmore

"If a learning community is to reach its goals and meet the needs of its students, the budget development process and final budget must reflect its priorities for the school."

—Marsha Speck

"A budget is an estimate, an educated guess, about revenue (income streams) and expenditures (disbursements of cash resources). That's all it is."

—John A. Black and Fenwick W. English

DeRoche (1987) outlines steps for establishing a school budget. As principal you should play an active role in each step. According to DeRoche (1987, p. 261), you should display knowledge and skill in the following areas:

- Understanding budget-making procedures
- Developing a school budget that results from consultation with faculty and staff
- Preparing a school budget that supports the school's educational program
- Keeping accurate financial records of receipts and expenditures
- Preparing and delivering sound financial reports to the superintendent, the board, and the school's public
- Effectively managing and evaluating budget allocations made to the school

Presumably, in your administrator graduate preparation program you took a course on budgeting and accounting or at least were exposed to several seminars and visited schools to observe the budget in process. Your best learning opportunity has come on your first job as principal, because there is nothing like learning from experience. The discussion that follows, based on the work of DeRoche (1987), provides "an overview designed to help you evaluate how to go about the task of budgeting, and how to skillfully administer and account for budget allocations" (p. 261). For each of DeRoche's three steps, I've raised relevant questions to keep in mind as you work on them.

Preparing the budget

- Are you familiar with the budget classification system used in your district or region?
- What are the basic budget categories you are expected to address?
- How do you use these categories in preparing your school's budget?

- How is the total school budget framed, and how does it relate to the larger district budget?
- In preparing the budget, do you consider the needs of students?
- In preparing the budget, do you consider the needs of teachers?
- In preparing the budget, do you consider the needs of staff?
- Have you considered how the budget will help you achieve the institutional mission?
- Have you considered how the budget will help you accomplish the strategic goals?
- Have you made a strong case for increasing the budget in various areas?
- How successful were you?
- What might you do differently next year?
- Have you asked teachers and your APs to provide rationales for their requests?
- Have you considered what items get priority over others?
- On what basis will you prioritize budget items?
- Will you make known your criteria for prioritization?
- Have you made cost estimates?
- Have you considered what you will do if the budget isn't approved?
- How was money spent last year?
- What cost savings measures have you taken in the past?

> *"Educational planning, the weighing of priorities and of alternative means to accomplish them, is the essential feature of budgeting in the schools."*
>
> —Carl Candoli, Walter G. Hack, and John R. Ray

Administering the budget

- Now that the budget has been approved, will you ensure that funds allotted to each area will be spent properly?
- What mechanism will you establish to ensure that monies are allocated for their intended purposes?
- How can you use technology to help administer the budget?
- Do you have accounting procedures established?
- Are you in constant communication with the central office?

- Have you established standard procedures for purchasing?
- Are you familiar with competitive bidding regulations?

Evaluating budget management

- How do you intend to evaluate budget management in your school?
- How will you know if monies have been inappropriately or even illegally spent?
- Have you consulted with the central office about their requirements for evaluating budget management?
- How will you conduct the annual audit?
- How will you plan for the audit?
- How well did you prepare the budget?
- How well have school funds been managed?
- How well have school supplies and equipment been managed?
- How have you involved faculty and staff in the budget process?
- Do you keep everyone informed about the budget periodically?

Reflective Questions

1. How might these questions guide you in handling the budget and in all financial matters?

2. Whom can you consult in your district to help you with questions you don't know the answer to?

This chapter will highlight varied ways you as the principal can effectively deal with school finance and budget issues. The information presented is concise and requires comparison with processes that exist in your school and district, because practices in these areas vary greatly from school to school and district to district. Also, please note that the descriptions in this chapter are of the ideal. In the real world, principals scramble, at times, to balance their budgets, and sometimes—some would say often—there is little room for creative budgeting.

> **What You Should Know About School Finance and Handling the Budget**
>
> - **Fiscal Fitness**—General ideas and concepts involved in school finance and budgeting are discussed.

1. FISCAL FITNESS

Explanation and caveat: This best practice is modeled after a book by Ramsey (2001) by the same title. You need to have some basic knowledge of the fiscal process as well as strategies or techniques for handling the budget. Therefore, this best practice represents the requisite knowledge every effective principal manager needs when dealing with finance and budget issues. Note that the discussion in this section is brief and general. See Resource C for additional readings and realize, above all else, that you'll learn much about fiscal issues on the job. Any book or description of finances and budgeting is limited, because practices and methods used from district to district and school to school vary enormously. Also note that some schools operate under a school-based budgeting process in which most decisions are made at the school level, although mandates do exist, such as the use of Title I funds (i.e., Title I set-asides). Other schools, like those in New York City for instance, have moved away from school-based budgeting to a more centralized and restrictive process in which principals are in charge of budgeting but have well-prescribed guidelines they must follow.

> *"Fiscal fitness is the state of operating at peak efficiency and productivity."*
>
> —Robert D. Ramsey

Some of you are charged with overseeing all financial matters in your school building, from allocating funds, to spending them in any way you deem appropriate (albeit within general parameters), to accounting for them, to managing the whole process. Others of you may have minimal involvement in budgetary matters. The national trend, however, is to give principals greater authority for expenditures, because, as front-line managers, principals are in the best position to make decisions that can positively influence student learning. However, preparing, administering, and working closely with central office administrators and external federal and state agencies is no easy task. Still, with this greater control over fiscal matters comes, of course, more accountability. Even in cases in which you are chiefly responsible, you likely have administrative support from central office accountants and other financial experts. You certainly are not expected to have sole expertise in these matters. Therefore, your knowledge of these fiscal matters need not be so detailed or extensive. As Drake and Roe (2003) affirm:

> We are not suggesting the principal needs to be a financial expert or accountant. But we do believe a practicing school administrator must be knowledgeable enough to keep on top of the school's budgeting and accounting process and to speak and understand the language. The principal should be able to participate on equal terms with central administrators when decisions that depend on the allocation of funds are being made. (p. 455)

As reflected in the Case Study earlier in this book, Ms. Valez, the principal, was very much aware that a budget is a financial plan that is ideally based on educational goals and objectives that reflect the shared commitment of the school community. The budget, in other words, is framed to financially support the school's mission. Budgeting requires educators to examine organizational needs to best meet the educational interests of students. Budgeting does not occur in isolation of a systematic plan to accomplish the school's goals and objectives. A principal, for instance, may decide to allocate funds to extend an ELL teacher's work from three to five days a week given the fact that the number of ELL children in the school has doubled over the course of the school year. Providing additional support to the ELL program is considered important to the extent to which it reflects school goals and objectives. The budget process therefore requires mindful attention to school needs based on the unique circumstances of a given school. In the aforementioned case, the significant increase in ELL students is a concern that needs direct attention.

Effective principals who address finance and budget issues possess unique skills:

- They are very well organized and can multitask.
- They have a keen understanding and awareness of their school's strengths and limitations.
- They affirm the school's mission and do everything they can to ensure its accomplishment.
- They are good financial planners and managers.
- They have a grounded sense of ethics and morality.
- They believe in social justice, equity, and opportunity for all people.
- They know what they want and how to get it.

Further, these principals "can examine a school budget and recognize important programs and the particular curriculum or staff development direction that a school is pursuing" (Alvy & Robbins, 1998, p. 63).

Two distinct methods or approaches to budgeting are commonplace:

- Line-item budgeting—This is the oldest and most commonly used method. In spreadsheet format, categories or types of expenditures are listed down the left column. For instance, some of the line items may include "Teacher Salaries," "Library Books," "Computer Equipment," "General Supplies," and so forth. Each of these budgetary categories may have a particular code or number associated with it (e.g., "100," Teacher Salaries; "200," Textbooks). After dealing with a budget or two, you will become familiar with the process, knowing, though, that codes may change from time to time. A second column lists the amount of monies allocated for each category, the third column lists amounts of expenditures, and a fourth column lists the amount remaining in the budget. Variations of this line-item process exist. Tracking expenditures and reallocation of funds (i.e., you can in some cases move monies from one category to another) is quite easy, and thus this method of budgeting is popular and common. In line-item budgeting, no explanation or purpose for categories or expenditures is provided.

- Program budgeting—In contrast to line-item budgeting, program budgeting includes program purpose or objectives with estimated expenditures listed by category. In effect, program budgeting includes line-item budgeting. One of the most common forms of such budgeting is known as Planning, Programming Budgeting System (PPBS). Proposals for various programs or initiatives are solicited and then scrutinized by those in authority in order to prioritize them, given the fact that monies are limited. Not everything can be funded, and so it is critical that the principal include others in the decision-making process to avoid conflicts and resentments that naturally occur when one program is funded over another. One of the chief complaints occurs as a result of not making known the criteria used in selecting one program over another. Another program budgeting method is known as Zero-Based Budgeting (ZBB). All budgets start with zero funds and require justification for allocation of funds. "The mere fact that a program was funded during the current year or in previous years is no assurance that it will be funded in subsequent years" (Ubben, Hughes, & Norris, 2004, p. 277). In contrast to ZBB, Incremental Budgeting, more commonly used because it's not as complicated, involves automatic incremental increases for all categories. With this sort of budgeting, "the principal will be expected to project needs for the next year on a formula that most often is based on the number of students anticipated to be enrolled" (Ubben et al., p. 277). The principal will have the opportunity, though, to request special new funds to fund new projects (e.g., building a new computer lab). Still, incremental budgeting is premised on the notion that needs from year to year remain constant. The disadvantage of such an approach is obvious. Some categories that are no longer viable may receive increases, whereas other categories with newer and greater demands may receive the same increase.

Reflective Question

1. What are some of the advantages and disadvantages to the budgeting methods or approaches just discussed?

Compare your responses of the Reflection Question above to the following information:

The line-item budget is simple to use and can be controlled or checked easily (both an advantage and disadvantage). Can you think under what circumstances it may be a disadvantage?

PPBS is systematic and tied to program objectives. Organizational goals are identified and then funded by leaders. In the ZBB process, funding begins from the ground up, but it requires detailed rationales for funding, which can be time-consuming. Site-based management teams are usually actively involved in the ZBB process. The teams continually reevaluate priorities. Incremental budgeting is automatic but not systematically evaluated.

Reflective Question

1. Which method of budgeting is used by your school or district?

Ubben et al. (2004) advocate the PPBS. According to these authorities (p. 278), PPBS involves five steps:

1. Establishing general goals to be achieved

2. Identifying the specific objectives that define this goal

3. Developing the program and processes that it is believed will achieve the objectives and goals

4. Establishing the formative and summative evaluation practices

5. Implementing a review and recycle procedure that indicates whether or not, or the degree to which, the program and processes resulted in the achievement of the objectives and the goals, and if not, helping to determine other procedures, processes, and programs

Other budgetary and financial concerns and items you should be aware of include the following, among others:

- Familiarity with all budgetary categories
- Remaining aware of new changes issued by federal, state, and local (district) agencies
- Deadlines and timelines
- Restricted allocations
- Allocations based on student attendance
- Cost estimates and biddings

- Monitoring student attendance tied to budget allocations
- Moving funds from one category to another (allowances and limitations)
- Federal, state, and local stipulations
- Familiarity with district policies and procedures at every step in the budget process
- Access to federal and state codes, rules, and regulations (a handbook)
- Reporting procedures to central office, school board, state agencies, and so on
- Participatory management of the budget
- Use of computer technology in handling the budget (hardware and software)
- Varied forms used for purchases, expenses, and so on
- Accounting procedures for budget categories
- Inventory keeping
- Vendor information
- Shortfalls and overexpenditures
- Use of other funds (e.g., grants, student activities, donations)

In some instances, you will be asked to present a rationale before funding is allocated by the central office or other agency. In other cases, allocations will be made independent of your input. From time to time, however, especially in times of economic crises, you will be asked to reduce your budget by a given percentage. How do you decide what should get reduced or cut, and what other guidelines should you follow in times of retrenchment? The following suggestions are paraphrased, in part, from Ramsey (2001):

- Reducing any budget in total or by category should be considered in light of the school's mission, including its goals and objectives, so that its integrity is assured.
- Involve others in determining cuts or reductions.
- Publicize prioritization criteria.
- Do not make cuts indiscriminately, because not all programs are of equal value.
- When cutting or reducing budget items, try to always do so as far away from affecting the classroom as possible.
- Assess the value of human versus material resources for a particular program or initiative.

- Adhere to contractual obligations and commitments.
- Try to scale back before having to cut completely.
- Determine if fund-raising initiatives can reduce further cutbacks.
- Carefully consider the consequences of any cutback.
- Prepare a backup list of cutbacks or reductions if the situation worsens.
- Consult your superintendent for advice prior to taking action.
- Be prepared to defend your decisions, and expect complaints.

Ramsey (2001) concludes with some succinct advice: "When difficult budget cuts are called for, effective principals put off procrastination. It won't get easier. It may get worse. Just do it" (p. 18).

Again, you need not serve as financial expert. Your school district undoubtedly has an individual or office devoted exclusively to all aspects of business management. These administrators serve to support your efforts. Getting to know them and soliciting their advice and input regularly is essential and very much advisable. In dealing with school finance and budgetary issues, you need not necessarily know very much about these topics, but a general familiarity of the following is advisable (Garner, 2004):

- Historical events associated with school finance
- Emerging developments (e.g., vouchers, charter schools)
- Policy-making issues beyond the school-building level
- Relationship between education and economics
- All federal and state court decisions related to education equity issues
- Advanced accounting procedures
- Identification of revenue and income sources
- Calculation of property tax assessments
- Selling of bonds to raise revenue
- Governmental accounting funds

Check Resource C for a suggested text that provides detailed information about these subjects.

Reflective Question

1. Visit with two principals you know who are very much involved in administering budgets. Compare their activities. Describe their budget processes. What similarities and differences exist?

CONCLUSION

School finance and school budgeting are best learned on the job, because practices and systems used vary so much. Attending workshops sponsored by your district and forming a close professional relationship with the chief business officer of your district are two necessary tasks you should undertake. Discussion in this chapter has been brief, general, and meant as an introduction to a complicated process that you will learn on the job.

CHAPTER FIVE

Best Practices in Human Resources Management

"School administrators are expected to know the law. The courts will not accept ignorance of the law as a defense."

—Dennis R. Dunklee and Robert J. Shoop

"Human resource theorists argue that the central task of managers is to build organizations and management systems that produce harmony between the needs of the individual and the needs of the organization."

—Lee G. Bolman and Terrence E. Deal

"Traditional bureaucratic approaches to organization and the newer approaches that emphasize the human dimensions of organization exist side by side and often compete for the attention and loyalty of educational administrators."

—Robert G. Owens

O perational leadership refers in large part to managing human interests and concerns within the school organization. It also relates to finding that fine balance between the needs of individuals and the organization, which was discussed in brief in the answer to some of the questions in the Questionnaire introduced earlier. According to Bolman and Deal (2000, p. 61), the human resources frame is built on the following assumptions:

1. Organizations exist to serve human needs (rather than the reverse).

2. Organizations and people need each other. (Organizations need ideas, energy, and talent; people need careers, salaries, and work opportunities.)

3. When the fit between the individual and the organization is poor, one or both will suffer; individuals will be exploited, or will seek to exploit the organization, or both.

4. A good fit between individual and organization benefits both: human beings find meaningful and satisfying work, and organizations get the human talent and energy that they need.

The essence of operational leadership, it seems to me, is the challenge to address this balance between individual interests and organizational mandates. For Dewey, the issue was even larger, because he saw it as a problem in education at large. For him, the problem of education was the "harmonizing of individual traits with social ends and values" (Mayhew & Edwards, 1965, p. 465). As principal, you are certainly committed to maintaining the structure of schooling. In fact, you are charged with the responsibility of gatekeeper or guardian of the institution. At the same time, you realize that the organization is made up of individuals. On the one hand, the organization represents the collective values and standards of all individuals who have ever worked in the organization, as well as societal norms and requirements that must be fulfilled. On the other hand, individuals currently in the organization shape the norms and values of the organization by virtue of their presence and commitment to the system. How do you balance these needs? There are situations in which the needs of the organization must reign supreme, as in a case involving, for instance, attendance requirements of personnel. If Jerry is continually late to work, although he may have a viable excuse in that his mother, whom he cares for on a daily basis, is quite ill, then his absence nevertheless has consequences for an orderly administration of the school day. Practically, his class needs coverage. Legal mandates require that students be supervised by licensed personnel. An added complication is that his students are losing out on valuable instructional time by his repeated tardiness or absences. Here's a case in which the organization requires adherence to standard procedures of operation (i.e., attendance policy), yet there are individual constraints (Jerry's need to care for his mother). As principal, you have to make a decision or take a course of action to address this problem.

> *"Leaders must be caring and supportive of people who work in schools but also must champion and protect the integrity and common good of the institution."*
>
> —Terrence E. Deal and Kent D. Peterson

The needs of the individual in this organization-individual engagement were addressed by Abraham Maslow. Maslow (1954) grouped human needs into five basic categories or groups. Arranged in a hierarchy, from low to high, lower needs must be satisfied before an individual strives for higher ones. Groupings include the following:

1. Physiological needs (such as needs for oxygen, water, food, physical health, and comfort)

2. Safety needs (to be safe from danger, attack, threat)

3. Belongingness and love needs (needs for positive and loving relationships with other people)

4. Needs for esteem (needs to feel valued and to value oneself)

5. Needs for self-actualization (needs to develop oneself fully, to actualize one's potential)

Building on Maslow's theory, McGregor (1960) "took Maslow's theory of motivation and added another central idea, namely, that the perspective from which a manager views other people determines how they respond" (Bolman & Deal, 2000, p. 64). According to McGregor, managers worked on the basis of what he called Theory X. The need for managers to direct and control their workers (subordinates) is fundamental to this theory. According to Theory X, "subordinates are passive and lazy, have little ambition, prefer to be led, and resist change" (p. 65). Theory Y, in contrast, asserts that individuals are naturally committed to doing good work in schools. According to McGregor (cited by Bolman & Deal, pp. 65–66), Theory Y is premised on the idea that "the essential task of management is to arrange organizational conditions so that people can achieve their own goals best by directing their efforts toward organizational rewards." According to this theory, people are self-reliant and intrinsically motivated to do the right thing. Put more simply by Bolman and Deal, "Theory X treats people like children, whereas Theory Y treats them like adults" (p. 66).

Reflective Questions

1. How would you deal with or resolve this organization-individual issue?

2. How does this issue relate to your role in operational management?

In spite of this organization-individual contrast, you as the principal must attend to a variety of human resource issues and concerns. The point here is that as you do so, you will inevitably have to address organizational and individual conflicts. This chapter will address a variety of human resource issues that fall under your responsibility as operational leader. Two primary questions to keep in mind when managing human resources issues are as follows (note that only the first question is usually posed in the literature):

- How do school people work to support organizational goals?
- How can the organization be structured to best support human interests?

I personally think that we need to conduct our work in schools from the vantage point of the latter question. Organizations cannot function as independent, monolithic "steel monsters," if you will, but must reflect individual aspirations, talents, and goals. That is not to suggest, of course, that all individual interests are worthy. Cultural norms and expectations, initiated by the interests and views of people, eventually become accepted practice within organizations. Aberrant behavior is unacceptable, and people should establish mechanisms to thwart unacceptable behaviors. Still, we must not lose sight of the fact that organizations were conceived, are maintained, and are renewed by . . . us.

Ideas or best practices in this chapter clearly focus around human resource issues. As principal, you realize you cannot accomplish your lofty goals without the input, assistance, and even the dedication of others. Rather than just presenting some rather dry information, as many textbooks on the subject do, about recruiting, selecting, retaining, and evaluating personnel, I thought that presenting each human resource idea within the context of a brief case study might serve to highlight the importance of these issues to a finer degree.

What You Should Know About Human Resources Management

- **Recruiting, Inducting, and Retaining Good Teachers**—Learn from Alicia Kaelber and her commitment to best practices in teaching.
- **Evaluating Personnel and Programs**—Learn how Donald Toscano goes about evaluating personnel and programs in his building.
- **Working With the Union**—Learn Dominec Reno's suggestions for working with the union.

- **Dealing With Conflict**—Learn how Nazim Selovic deals with conflict.
- **Working With Your Assistant Principal**—Learn how Ronald Davis works with his three APs.
- **Attending to Legal Mandates**—Learn about the suggestions offered Fernando Montalvo by his mentor.
- **Promoting In-Classroom and Schoolwide Positive Student Behavior**—Learn Teresa Radzik's advice for supporting appropriate student behavior schoolwide.

1. RECRUITING, INDUCTING, AND RETAINING GOOD TEACHERS

Alicia Kaelber, principal of Brockton Elementary in a rural midwestern community, is experienced, with more than 15 years as principal in the same school. "Ms. Kaelber has gained in popularity within her school community over the years," states her superintendent. "She is beloved by faculty, staff, parents, and students alike because she really cares about what she considers her most important duty as building principal; i.e., attracting the very best teachers and staff for her school." When a local newspaper interviewed Ms. Kaelber about her philosophy of leading and managing, she unabashedly and assertively put it this way: "All the focused energy of a school should be harnessed to accomplish one thing and one thing only, to provide the highest and best education for all our children so that each and every one of them can achieve their potential as human beings in order to become contributing members of society." She continued, after being asked by the reporter how one could accomplish such a lofty goal: "And the only way to actualize such a goal is to attract, train, and retain the very best teachers because it is the teacher, not I or you as parent, that has the single greatest influence on the education of that child. Not that we play a mean role, we all are important, but learning and achievement start in the classroom."

Alicia Kaelber knows what she wants from a teacher. She wants teachers who are first and foremost caring, empathetic, and ethical human beings who really consider teaching a calling. Speaking to a group of prospective and new teachers, she passionately said:

Extraordinary times call for extraordinary teachers. We need teachers who can challenge others to excellence, teachers who love what they do. We need teachers who help students achieve their potential, teachers who help students understand why and how to treat others with respect, dignity, and compassion.

Haim Ginott (1993) made the point that education is more than teaching knowledge and skills in dramatic fashion when he related a message sent by a principal to his teachers on the first day of school:

Dear Teacher:

I am a survivor of a concentration camp. My eyes saw what no man should witness:

Gas chambers built by *learned* engineers.

Children poisoned by *educated* physicians.

Infants killed by trained nurses.

Women and babies shot and burned by *high* school and *college* graduates.

So, I am suspicious of education.

My request is: Help your students become human. Your efforts must never produce learned monsters, skilled psychopaths, educated Eichmanns.

Reading, writing, arithmetic are important only if they serve to make our children more humane. (p. 317)

The challenges of teaching are certainly awesome. Overcrowded classrooms, lack of student interest, absenteeism, lack of preparedness, high incidence of misbehavior, lack of parental support compounded by social problems such as drugs, unstable family life, teenage pregnancy, poverty, child abuse, violence and crime give pause to think. But think again. If not for these challenges the rewards of teaching would not be so great. Our work matters. You make a difference.

Yet Alicia Kaelber realizes that great teachers possess much more. She wants classroom teachers who are competent, who possess the necessary knowledge and skills of good pedagogy. More specifically, she looks for teachers who share the school's mission and passion for inclusive education. "It takes a special and gifted teacher to fit in and work here," she explains. "We need teachers who believe that all children can learn but not in the same way every day. Teachers need to be able to address the unique talents of each child. Therefore, they must possess skills in differentiated instruction, learning styles, and using multiple intelligences theory." She goes on, "In my school we don't separate certified special education students from the general population. We believe that it is indeed possible to educate all children within the confines of one classroom. We don't mainstream, we include. We don't pull out, we push in. We provide the services and resources necessary for teachers to succeed with all students. As such, teachers must adhere to such a pedagogical approach and be willing to team-teach, coteach, and collaborate with others."

Ms. Kaelber puts her goals into action by actively seeking teachers who match her ideals. "She is uncompromising," explains the superintendent. "We can't place a teacher in her school who simply wants a transfer closer to her home. If a teacher doesn't possess the knowledge, skills, and dispositions that match her ideal, she will not accept that teacher under any circumstances. We've had many battles with union officials, but to her credit, Ms. Kaelber doesn't back off. Others respect her assertive commitment to what she believes in."

Ms. Kaelber engages in the following activities to attract "the very best teachers" into her school:

- Attends every teaching fair or hiring hall she possibly can
- With help of the PTA, places ads in local and other papers specifying the kinds of teachers she's looking for
- Partners with the local college that prepares teacher candidates and offers her school as a site for field observations prior to student teaching and for student teaching itself
- Supports Professional Development School initiatives to "grow your own" teachers
- Offers open houses for teacher candidates so that they can learn about her school and so that she and others can learn about the candidates
- Looks carefully at every student teacher to determine if a "star" can be found
- Interviews prospective teachers using a team approach and asks the better candidates to conduct a demonstration lesson in front of a real class

- Asks each candidate to talk about education, while Ms. Kaelber listens for evidence reflecting an ethic of caring for children and the possession of skills to help each child learn
- Spends a great deal of time, sometimes half a day, with a likely candidate to be able to get to know the prospect better
- Provides a comprehensive report to the superintendent for each teacher she wants to hire, detailing the reasons why the candidate is a good match for her school

Ms. Kaelber realizes the importance of hiring a good teacher, but she also realizes that a teacher is not a completed product. "Every one of us must continue to learn and grow. We too often hire a teacher and let her flounder. Not in my school," she asserts. "We offer each candidate extensive training at a retreat prior to the school year conducted in large measure by the more experienced teachers at the school. Each new hire, regardless of experience level, is paired with a mentor. Staff development in my school is not episodic but built in to everything we do." Ms. Kaelber prides herself on the ongoing, meaningful, teacher-initiated, and well-run professional development programs that offer support for every teacher at her or his level of experience and need. "Our induction program for new hires is something we take pride in," she explains. "We work hard to support and retain all our good teachers." Ms. Kaelber is directly involved in leading and managing these initiatives in the following ways:

- Solicits funds (grants, donations, etc.) and, if unavailable, utilizes funds from her allocated budget for training and induction programs, because she feels that such money is well spent
- Plans weekend retreats throughout the school year on and away from school grounds
- Personally selects mentors for each new hire
- Schedules time for mentors and mentees to meet during the school day
- Organizes staff and professional development sessions throughout the school year
- Contacts local college professors to offer workshops in her school on selected topics based on needs of faculty
- Works closely with central office administrators to provide additional training for her faculty

- Works with the budget to ensure that enough monies are allocated to support innovative teaching ideas
- Orders appropriate equipment and supplies to support her teachers
- Personally meets with each teacher for extended periods of time to listen to concerns and provide constructive feedback
- Doesn't focus her efforts only on new hires, but is concerned with teachers who have 5, 10, 15, and 20 years of teaching experience
- Manages and oversees all aspects of induction and retention of teachers

---

Reflective Questions

1. Which of Alicia Kaelber's practices make the most sense to you?

2. How is she able to devote so much time to such initiatives?

3. What specific strategy or strategies that you do not currently use might be helpful in your school?

4. What other management strategies could Ms. Kaelber employ to help in recruiting, inducting, and retaining teachers?

5. What organization-individual issue, as discussed earlier in this chapter, is raised in this case study with Ms. Kaelber?

---

2. EVALUATING PERSONNEL AND PROGRAMS

One of the chief management responsibilities of Mr. Donald Toscano is evaluation. "I realize that as chief manager and leader of my school, I must above all else remain committed to the school organization and ensure the highest standards of accountability." "We may want all teachers and staff to succeed," explains this middle school principal in an urban area on the West Coast, "but we must equally realize that not all can despite our efforts to assist them. We are first and foremost responsible to ensure that our students have only the best. I take my evaluative duties very seriously."

Mr. Toscano, a veteran principal, understands the difference between evaluation and supervision. "Put simply, I see supervision as that process that facilitates instructional dialogue so that teachers begin and continue to reflect on best teaching practices with the aim to promote student achievement. Evaluation, on the other hand and to my mind," he continues, "has little if any instructive value other than to point out areas that need improvement. Evaluation, for me, is to ensure accountability; i.e., do we have competent and satisfactory personnel performing at acceptable levels, within and outside the classroom?" He adds:

> I undertake the evaluation process to collect data that will inform my decision making. What approaches does Ms. Smith need to improve her work? How have I mentored or counseled her to achieve success? Have I put her on notice, in writing, of deficiencies that are unsatisfactory and unacceptable? Does she have the ability to meet my expectations for success? If not, what can and should I do to remove her from her position?

Evaluation, for Mr. Toscano and others like him, is not a pleasant duty, but it is certainly necessary. Mr. Toscano is involved in the following two areas of evaluation: personnel and programs.

• Personnel Evaluation—Performance appraisal systems vary across the country. Various evaluative systems or approaches have been advocated over the years. Each school or district may vary its approaches based on contractual obligations and other factors. Mr. Toscano fully understands how his school district mandates personnel evaluation. All new first-year teachers must be formally observed three times, with written and documented letters placed in the teacher's file. A satisfactory or unsatisfactory rating is awarded at the end of the year. All untenured teachers (those with less than three years' experience) can be summarily fired at any time within the three years. Although the principal must submit documented reasons for firing a teacher, few if any district principals have been made to justify new teacher dismissals. As an experienced principal, Mr. Toscano documents all his evaluations in writing, because he recalls what a professor mentor once taught him: "If it ain't in writing, it never happened."

Mr. Toscano uses the district-mandated checklist form at given intervals throughout the school year. Mr. Toscano conducts both announced and unannounced classroom visits to untenured teachers. He meets with each teacher in a post conference to share his reactions and then sends the teacher a formal letter detailing the discussion. Specific recommendations are made for improvement, with professional development activities suggested. It is the teacher's responsibility to follow through, and Mr. Toscano always revisits the teacher's classroom. Some of Mr. Toscano's activities and responsibilities for personnel evaluation include the following:

1. Organized and systematic evaluation procedures

2. Scheduled observations throughout school year

3. Master calendar or schedule kept

4. Evaluation procedures discussed and shared with faculty and personnel

5. Faculty meetings planned to discuss evaluation procedures and processes

6. Individual conferences throughout school year with faculty and staff to discuss evaluative reports

7. Forms for district office completed and submitted in time

Remember, you have no greater authority and responsibility as a principal than to hire the best and fire the worst. Do not accept mediocrity, but certainly incompetence is anathema. Do all you can to document efforts to assist the incompetent. Be sure to put your evaluations honestly in writing. If someone deserves an "unsatisfactory," give it. Start the documentation process to remove the teacher, as difficult as it may be to do so for a tenured teacher. Always keep in mind the children. Would you want that teacher teaching your child or grandchild? Don't praise someone who doesn't deserve the accolade. It'll come back to haunt you.

> "The test of leadership is to be able to extend to teachers an invitation to accept responsibility for themselves, and to have them accept it."
>
> —Thomas J. Sergiovanni

Reflective Questions

1. What does "If it ain't in writing, it never happened" mean?

2. Why do you think Mr. Toscano meets individually with each faculty and staff member after each evaluation?

- Program Evaluation—Program evaluation is included under human resource management, because programs are run by people, and we cannot divorce program effectiveness from people effectiveness. How effective a program is or is not may be reflective of the people assigned to manage the program. Mr. Toscano affirms what Sanders (2000) has stated: "Successful program development cannot occur without evaluation. Program evaluation is the process of systematically determining the quality of a school program and how the program can be improved" (p. 3). As principal, Mr. Toscano has to manage and administer various educational and noneducational programs. He asks himself these questions:

1. Do I fully understand how to conduct evaluation research?
2. Do I possess the skills to conduct evaluation research on my own?
3. Have I undertaken an extensive review of a program in my school within the last year?
4. Do I understand the difference between formative and summative evaluation?
5. Do I believe that data must be collected from a variety of sources in any program evaluation?
6. Can I conduct a program evaluation on my own without assistance from others?

Mr. Toscano first asks himself, "What is evaluation research?" He knows that evaluation research is the gathering of data in order to make a decision. He makes many decisions on a daily basis. Unfortunately, many of these decisions are sometimes made hurriedly and without the scrutiny of thoughtful, scientific investigation. What seems to be most expedient at the time is often the most important criterion for determining, for example, the fate of a new music program. Based on his experiences in schools, he has found that when principals are trained in sound action research methodology, decisions are made more intelligently and equitably. To determine the "fate of the new music program," he knows he needs to collect appropriate data from a number of sources before making the final decision to disband, modify, or continue the music program. The value of evaluation research, he acknowledges, is its ability to help him make informed and intelligent educational decisions.

He asks himself questions such as these: "Does the new program work?" "What impact does inclusion have on the attitudes of teachers?" and "Does the Balanced Literacy program affect reading achievement levels among third graders?" He acknowledges that "program evaluation that is regular, dynamic, and ongoing contributes greatly to the overall effectiveness of the school organization."

A very common form of decision making is known as procedural evaluation. Evaluation of this nature is concerned with examining school procedures such as safety plans, scheduling, emergencies, supply distributions, and so forth. His AP can assist in this process. He and his AP need to evaluate facilities and equipment, financial plans, school resources, and instructional materials on an ongoing basis. His district office has special forms that he must use for evaluation. Under the leadership of the new superintendent, in-building evaluations will return to the discretion of the principal. Mr. Toscano expects that he will have to devise his own forms for such evaluations. He intends to establish an evaluation committee that includes custodial and other staff members to collaborate to develop evaluation criteria that are fair and consistently used.

Mr. Toscano has already developed a well-thought-out process for evaluating programs. He knows the evaluation should include a review of stated goals and accomplishment of those goals. He also knows he needs to assess various administrative or logistical aspects of the program, such as the following:

- Staffing considerations
- Scheduling
- Advertising
- Room allocations
- Ordering materials and supplies
- Securing funding sources and publicity
- Delegating responsibilities

In a nutshell, he wants to answer two fundamental questions:

- How are we doing?
- And how can we improve?

Mr. Toscano keeps in mind these three items:

- Evaluation is a comprehensive, ongoing process.

- Evaluation is formative and summative. Assessing progress along the way is imperative. Why wait six months or a year before realizing that changes are warranted? Formative evaluation allows for program adjustments and modifications. Research has indicated that programs that incorporate formative evaluative measures are more likely to succeed. Summative evaluation leads to one of three recommendations: (a) modification of program or procedure, (b) elimination of program or procedure, or (c) continuation of program or procedure.

- What should be assessed or evaluated? All programs, practices, and procedures should be evaluated, including, among others, school goals and objectives, parent-teacher conferences, assessment procedures (including report cards), faculty meetings, assembly programs, music programs, administrative procedures, dropout rates, attendance policies, schoolwide discipline plans, curriculum materials, pupil achievement, accounting procedures, and school climate.

How should he evaluate? He keeps this mnemonic in mind: *ROTC.*

R = Records and rating scales—examine records, develop rating or attitudinal surveys, and checklists

O = Observations, both formal and informal

T = Tests, standardized or nonstandardized

C = Conferences with everyone

He develops a general evaluation plan. In developing this plan, he keeps in mind these points:

1. What is the purpose of evaluation?

2. What needs to be evaluated?

3. What are our goals?

4. How will data be collected?

5. How will data be organized and analyzed?

6. How will the data be reported?

He realizes that problems are inevitable in program evaluation. Mr. Toscano keeps in mind these five steps for solving problems:

1. Analyze the situation.

2. Examine research (data collected or evidence).

3. Examine results.

4. Develop alternative solutions.

5. Act (modify, discard, or continue).

Reflective Questions

1. What are your reactions to Mr. Toscano's efforts to evaluate programs in his school?

2. What else might you include in the evaluation?

3. Have you ever undertaken a formal program evaluation? If so, what caveats might you recommend to novice principals?

---

3. WORKING WITH THE UNION

Dominec Reno is politically savvy. He learned the hard way, though. As an experienced high school principal in a large inner-city school in the Northeast, he has had many experiences dealing with union issues. He acknowledges the many mistakes he's made, but he says he learned much from those experiences. Asked by his superintendent to give a keynote presentation at the annual district affair, Dominec decides to share his experiences with the less experienced principals by organizing his talk in the form of practical suggestions for working with the union:

- Show respect. "Respect the right of all employees to unionize. Unions have a long history in our nation, and teachers have the right to have their interests safeguarded. Don't disparage or harbor resentment against a teacher for following union advice; it's their right. Understand and respect their rights."

- Avoid naïveté. "Don't say, 'Well, I'm a nice principal and fair to everyone, so there's no need for teachers to seek counsel from union officials. My door is always open. I believe in democracy, and everyone has the opportunity to work things out with me without having to resort to grievances.' Long ago, I too was that naive to assume simply good human relations will do the trick. We cannot get blindsided by the avoidance of politics. Politics is very much part of our professional lives. Accept and understand it. Being friendly and cordial to everyone is always a good idea, but don't think that your 'good looks' alone will prevent a teacher from seeking union counsel or initiating a grievance. Unions have their own momentum and inertia. They exert influence on their members regardless of your relationship with them."

- Avoid the "us" versus "them" mentality. "Unions are structured in reality to serve the interests of employees, not employers. Union officials will professionally interact with management but never forget who they serve. Even so, if you truly appreciate and respect teacher rights to unionize, then you will not look at the issue as antagonistic. You know that you are working for one purpose and for one purpose only, and that it is to help children learn. People of goodwill and conscience will naturally differ in their approaches. Accept that and always seek resolution. This resolution, however, must always, in the end, favor students, which brings me to my next point."

- Remain steadfast in your convictions. "Never compromise your strongly held convictions that affirm the dignity and success of your clients, the students. Negotiation and compromise are fine as long as you are not a wimp to the values you espouse. Giving in to union pressure that might mean, in your estimation, a diminution of student opportunities for excellence in learning should be avoided. Although others may contest you, they'll respect you in the end as a person of courage, willing to stand by his [or her] convictions."

• Collective bargaining is part of a democratic process. "Union-management relations can be strained at times, especially over contentious issues such as salary, benefits, and working conditions. Collective bargaining is a process that epitomizes the union-management relationship, that involves negotiating on a variety of issues. Bargaining is part of this process; accept it as a reality. As principal, you represent interests of management, they represent employee interests. We hope, of course, that the two interests are mutual. More often than not, unfortunately, interests are different. Again, I naively thought, 'Well, why can't we just get along?' My experience has taught me, we can, but we must adhere to this process. Sometimes, the needs and interests of individuals might necessarily conflict with organizational needs. You represent the organization; you are management, and don't forget that fact. Try for compromise in the best interests of all, but sometimes the political process may have to play out, which leads me to my next suggestion."

• Don't go it alone. "Seek counsel and advice from colleagues. More experienced principals can advise you on many issues you'll likely confront or are currently facing. Be deliberate in judgment; don't rush. Seek advice from someone you trust."

• Don't fear grievances. "I've known principals who can't stand behind their principles. They have few grievances because they continually give in to teachers on important issues to the organization. Grievances should be viewed as a teacher's right to formally air complaints and disputes. Don't forget that teachers might have their right to support what they think is best for themselves and the organization, but so do you. You are the gatekeeper for the organization. Sometimes interests may collide. You may be wrong at times, but they may be as well. Learn the grievance steps or process in your school district well. Read the contract and be able to quote chapter and verse. Learn from your colleagues. Ask questions. There's nothing for experience like going through a complete grievance hearing and decision process. Whenever you can, however, try to reach consensus to resolve the grievances.

Open lines of communication between teachers and administrators. Too many grievances may indicate poor communication. Still, some grievances are inevitable, so don't fear them. Prepare yourself."

• Meet with union officials. "Always keep channels of communication open. Schedule regular meetings with union leaders. Discuss problems that might arise, but also discuss projects that both the union (teachers) and administration can collaborate [on] for the benefit of students."

Reflective Questions

1. What are your reactions to Dominec Reno's suggestions for working with the union? What did you agree or disagree with?

2. What suggestions that he did not discuss would you raise?

3. How do these issues relate to our earlier discussion of organization-versus-individual matters?

---

4. DEALING WITH CONFLICT

Nazim Selovic works as principal in a middle school that has witnessed enormous staff turnover. Many conflicts occurred under the tenure of the former principal, who recently retired. Teachers and administration argued constantly, and conflicts among teachers were rampant. The culture of the school had grown over the years into an uncomfortable, unsympathetic, and at times even hostile environment in large measure because of the confrontational approach of the former principal. Mr. Selovic, brought in as principal from another district, had his work cut out for him. Yet, within a relatively short period of time, three years, he transformed the school into a nurturing learning community that now attracted teachers into the school. Retention increased tenfold, and morale was high.

Nazim Selovic, speaking before fellow administrators at a national conference, explained his success. Excerpts of his speech are quoted as follows:

"Conflict in schools is inevitable. Human nature dictates that people sometimes differ in viewpoints and may not get along with each other. People differ in temperaments. You must appreciate and even cherish the differences we each bring to our school.

"For me, working with Ms. Cummings was challenging, to say the least. She attempted, or so it seemed to me, to thwart my efforts as a new principal every step of the way. As a tenured teacher, she seemed to have a very different idea of the direction in which our school should go. Although I was principal, she challenged my decisions at every opportunity. It seemed to me that she would purposely spread rumors about me, although I could never substantiate her attempts to do so. I had a gut reaction, and I can read people well, usually. I was at my wits' end. How was I going to manage her and the situation?

"I tried to resolve situations that would arise by asking her to meet with me. She always complied, and it seemed our conversations went well, but as soon as the meeting was over, things stayed the same or even worsened. I tried the human relations approach, but nothing seemed to work with Ms. Cummings, and quite honestly, I [had] had it. I realized at one point that I could do nothing to improve our professional relationship. I realized then, perhaps for the first time, strange as it may seem, that some people just don't get along, and a separation would be necessary. I must say that I really could not do anything legally to oust her, since she was a tenured teacher with a fairly good record over her 18 years in the school. So, I put the pressure on her. I don't say I'm proud of what I did, but I knew that for my sanity and the future of my work in the school I had to take action. I utilized every rightful action using my authority as principal to 'make life difficult for her at the school.' Giving her 'special' patrol duties that, for instance, the former principal would never have given her, given the fact that she was a powerhouse in the school. Despite her complaints to me about the assignments I had given her, I remained steadfast and continued the pressure. She had not been formally observed in many years, but that now changed. I made certain that every move I made was done in an equitable manner. That is, I did not make it appear I was singling her out. To make a long story shorter, my day was made, I have to admit, when I reported to school one morning to find a notice on my desk that Ms. Cummings had requested a voluntary transfer out of the district based on what she wrote as a 'transportation hardship transfer.' She also attached a letter requesting a temporary leave of absence in order to try out the new position at the other school. I wrote her back that I would not allow her to take a one-year leave of absence. Either she would return to this school now or take the other position without the chance of returning to this school in the future. She opted for the latter.

"This case is not the norm, I am sure. Still, it does indicate the tough jobs we have with some individuals and the steps we sometimes have to take to manage the situation. More often than not, though, we deal with conflict between and among people daily. Most disagreements and conflicts can be worked out with reasonable measures over time. Here are some suggestions I can offer for managing conflicts among people who work in our schools:

- "Understand that conflicts and disagreements are a natural occurrence in all organizations.
- "Developing a learning community does not mean that people can't disagree; in fact, opportunities and forums to air and discuss disagreements [are] very much part of being a learning community; i.e., we all can learn from each other.
- "As managers, we must learn conflict resolution strategies [or] have systems or mechanisms in place in our schools so that conflicts are heard and resolved in a reasonable and collaborative manner.
- "Depending on the situation, we must be ready and able to make alterations in scheduling or general management procedures to accommodate differences among people.
- "Familiarize yourself with conflict resolution resources, including these Web sites: http://www.crnhq.org/; http://v4.crinfo.org/; and http://conflict.colorado.edu/, among others."

> "Successful school administrators ought to have excellent verbal and interpersonal skills."
>
> —Georgia J. Kosmoski and Dennis R. Pollack

Reflective Questions

1. What are your reactions to Nazim Selovic's suggestions for dealing with conflict? What did you agree or disagree with?

2. What suggestions that he did not discuss would you raise?

3. What is your reaction to how he dealt with Ms. Cummings?

4. How do these issues relate to our earlier discussion of organization-versus-individual matters?

5. WORKING WITH YOUR ASSISTANT PRINCIPAL

Ronald Davis is a veteran principal of a large elementary school in an urban area. His K–5 school has nearly 1,500 students, and so he has three APs who work with and for him. Here are some commonsense tips Mr. Davis has given for working with APs:

- Realize that each AP has something unique to offer the school.
- Discover the talent of each AP.
- Capitalize on the unique talents of each AP.
- Assign APs a grade level or responsibilities that will challenge them but will also give them the opportunity to succeed.
- Meet with them collectively as part of your cabinet, but also afford time for each one to see or meet with you privately.
- Realize that they are your "assistants," and as such, they are there to carry out your policies and to take leadership responsibilities in the areas you delegate to them.
- Listen to them, and solicit their advice regularly.
- Don't show favoritism to one over the other.
- Don't talk about one to another, especially in a negative way.
- Protect and support your APs.
- Understand and accommodate your AP's leadership style.

- Remain assertive by requesting them to assume leadership responsibilities in special areas.
- Assign each of them managerial duties to help alleviate your burdens, but don't give them work you'd never do.
- Do not make any major decision without seeking the assistance or advice of your APs.
- Praise them in public, and chastise them if necessary in private, individually.
- Remain honest by openly sharing your views of instructional improvement with your APs.
- Remain honest by openly sharing your views of management with your APs.
- Never criticize or question the authority of your AP in public.
- Offer to assist your AP in instructional, curricular, and administrative matters.
- Understand your APs' strengths and limitations, and offer to assist where and when necessary.
- Remain steadfast in your beliefs and share them with your APs.
- Offer to cover a lunch duty or some other mundane administrative assignment from time to time.
- Let them represent you at various district forums, when appropriate.
- Offer concrete proposals to maximize their performance.
- Share teacher views with the APs.
- Seek, in private, a rationale for their decisions.
- Respectfully demand their allegiance and loyalty to you, because you are ultimately responsible to the parents and children you serve.
- Serve as a mentor for them.
- Encourage innovative thinking.
- Encourage the advancement of their careers.
- Always see them as partners, your assistants.

In closing, your relationships with other people in the school system should also be carefully monitored (e.g., secretarial and custodial staff, superintendent and other central office administrators).

Reflective Questions

1. What are your reactions to the suggestions offered by Ronald Davis?

2. What other suggestions could you offer?

3. What is one problem you've had with an AP? Explain how you've attempted to resolve the problem.

4. How would you manage your school without an AP?

---

6. ATTENDING TO LEGAL MANDATES

Fernando Montalvo is not very law savvy, but he tries to read Perry Zirkel's "Court Side" column in the *Kappan* monthly. Fascinated with the complexities of the law, Fernando, a newly assigned principal at a local high school, recalls some discussion of the legal aspects of education in a graduate course he took toward certification as a school building principal. He cannot, however, remember much of what was discussed about legal concerns in education. Speaking one afternoon to his mentor, Fernando shared his discomfort in lacking knowledge of the law. Here are some suggestions that Fernando's mentor offered:

- Most principals beginning the job are similarly disadvantaged in that they know very little about legal matters and education.

- Obtain and skim some of the legal documents that exist in the school and in the district office.

- Keep as a reference any legal review documents recommended by your superintendent, and use as a resource as needed.

- Maintain close contact with the district legal officer, sometimes serving as deputy superintendent.

- Seek counsel whenever you have a question about a legal matter.

> "Principals are encouraged to stay current with the law through their professional associations and through professional development opportunities."
>
> —Jennifer A. Sughrue and
> M. David Alexander

- Even though, as principal, you conserve the status quo, trying to ensure a safe school environment, try to avoid being so restrictive in your interpretation of the law that you infringe on the rights of others (e.g., students, parents, and teachers).

- Principals are not expected to serve as legal experts.

- Principals, however, are expected to know some legal basics, including the following facts about the legal framework for public education:

  Fact: Federal, state, and local governments exert control over public education.

  Fact: Although education is a state responsibility via the 10th Amendment to the U.S. Constitution, the feds have historically exercised control over education matters when issues involve a particular crisis or national interest.

  Fact: The federal government in noted Supreme Court cases has addressed issues related to freedom of speech, student rights, discrimination in the workplace, students with disabilities, religion, and so on.

  Fact: States have played an enormous role in shaping education policy via state statutes or topics, among others, certification, contracts, tenure laws, dismissal procedures, race and gender discrimination, sexual harassment, age and other discrimination, negligence, corporal punishment, search and seizures, and so forth.

  Fact: Local boards of education have the right to determine day-to-day school policies that are not in violation of any state or federal mandates.

- Attend any workshops offered by your district office or local college seminar on the law and education.

• Again, whenever you are confronted with a possibly volatile issue that involves some legality, seek counsel before taking any action. The law is most often not cut and dried. There's much room for interpretation. Your actions may be construed by others as illegal. To be on safe ground, seek counsel from central office staff or personnel designated as legal experts. For instance, don't rely on court decisions that have affirmed searches of students in which reasonable suspicion exists for drug possession. The key word in the last sentence is reasonable. What may seem reasonable to you might not to a parent of the student. Seek counsel whenever possible.

• Experience is a good teacher. You will likely encounter many situations involving such matters as drug testings, child abuse, school prayer, dispensation of medicine, and student confidentiality issues (i.e., FERPA). Your experiences with these matters will serve as a basis on which to act in the future. Still, laws change, so keeping current with the latest statutes is critical to your success and longevity as principal.

• As a general source for your reference, I recommend one of the best resources on the topic. Read Dunklee and Shoop's (2006) work, and keep it on your desk.

Quoting Ubben et al. (2004), Fernando's mentor said:

A working knowledge about the legal principles, important court decisions, and current law is essential. Understanding the laws governing the operation of schools is important— not just in order to stay out of court but also, and importantly, to provide the kind of orderly, productive, and humane school basic to the continuation of a democratic society. (pp. 369–370)

Reflective Question

1. What other suggestions can you make regarding the law and education?

7. PROMOTING IN-CLASSROOM AND SCHOOLWIDE POSITIVE STUDENT BEHAVIOR

Teresa Radzik, principal of PS 998, takes her responsibility as chief school manager seriously. She is committed to nurturing and encouraging an orderly and disciplined school environment so that all students can achieve their best and teachers can work at their optimal levels. She affirms Cotton's (2003) research:

> Effective principals bring about this kind of environment by exhibiting personal warmth and accessibility, ensuring that there is a broad-based agreement about standards for student behavior, communicating high behavioral standards to students, seeking input from students about behavior policies, applying rules consistently from day to day and from student to student, delegating disciplinary authority to teachers, and providing in-school suspension accompanied by support for seriously disruptive students. (p. 8)

She knows that teaching is a challenging, complex art and science that demands not only knowledge and skill but also empathy, caring, and commitment. Frequently frustrating and exhausting, good teaching, she realizes, encourages, inspires, and arouses that latent spark within each student. Still, teachers are confronted with difficult, seemingly insurmountable obstacles that can be puzzling and exasperating. Student misbehavior, for instance, may drive a teacher to the very limits of his or her endurance.

She knows that the principles and practices of effective discipline and classroom management are among the most important professional concerns that practicing educators confront daily. She remains committed to providing teachers the support they need to encourage appropriate student behavior. She is ready, willing, and able to provide ongoing workshops and professional development to all teachers on topics including behavior modification, discipline with dignity, cooperative discipline, assertive discipline, and much more. She knows that she must support teachers in the classroom by enforcing a schoolwide discipline plan. Therefore, she is involved in the following activities:

- Conducts frequent workshops for teachers on classroom management and discipline
- Reviews school expectations for behavior and challenges teachers to include them in their classroom plans
- Supports teachers in adhering to their plans (e.g., if a student is legitimately sent to the principal's office, she makes sure the teacher's actions are supported by reprimanding the student and taking appropriate action rather than making the student a monitor)
- Monitors student compliance to classroom and schoolwide rules and procedures (e.g., conducts assemblies)
- Conducts thorough investigation of a discipline infraction, making sure to gather all facts before arriving at a decision
- Ensures that every teacher has developed and implemented a sound discipline plan

Ms. Radzik also adheres to many of the principles for implementing a schoolwide behavioral program suggested by Alvy and Robbins (1998), which include, among others:

- The idea that good instruction is key toward an effective behavioral strategy
- The notion that students must be allowed to take responsibility for their own actions as well as the consequences for them
- A zero-tolerance policy for school violence, in which suspensions and expulsions are not withheld when appropriate
- Schoolwide guidelines continually discussed with faculty at grade and faculty conferences, with very specific rules and procedures adhered to by the entire faculty, fully understanding that individual teachers may implement their own regulations but that a common understanding for appropriate behavior exists schoolwide
- The idea that a crisis or emergency plan exists and is reviewed continuously
- Early identification of students who exhibit antisocial behaviors so that referrals can be made to guidance counselors, school psychologists, social workers, parents, district office administrators, and even police, when appropriate
- Security measures updated and reviewed monthly

- Student activities program ongoing and monitored
- Student guidance services active
- Partnerships with community to support student behavior (e.g., Big Brothers and Big Sisters, YMCA, drug agencies)

Principals have to manage a great deal in schools. But management of student behavior should not be avoided, because it supports excellence in instruction, which promotes student learning and achievement. Therefore, management of schoolwide disciplinary issues indirectly affects student achievement, a task and responsibility we must never ignore.

Reflective Question

1. What are other suggestions you can make regarding managing student behavior schoolwide?

CONCLUSION

Human resources management, or working with people, is a huge part of your work as principal. Unless you are a "people person," willing to interact in positive ways with others, you are destined to fail. Managing book orders, overseeing facilities building, and administering the budget are important, but they generally do not involve intense work with people. To remain effective in your role as principal, you must devote sufficient time to managing the human resources aspect of your job. This chapter has addressed only some of your responsibilities in this area. Your continued work in this area is very much needed. As principal, you may manage things, but your ability to manage people in all facets of schoolwork is critical to your success as operational leader.

CHAPTER SIX

Best Practices in Communicating Effectively

"True communication occurs when the listener hears what the sender intends."

—Rodney J. LaBrecque

"When people engage in effective communication with one another, they authentically share information and construct meaning together."

—Randall B. Lindsey, Laraine M. Roberts, and Franklin CampbellJones

"The principalship is a 'people' profession, and no degree of expertise in instructional, curricular, budgetary, or time management skills is going to make principals successful if they lack the ability to communicate honestly with students, faculty, classified staff, parents, and the broader community."

—Harvey B. Alvy and Pam Robbins

My grandfather, may he rest in peace, used to say, "The most important ingredient for a successful marriage is good communication." Communication is certainly essential in our interpersonal relationships. A couple that communicates ineffectively may jump to conclusions needlessly or may grow isolated from one another over time. Communication is also necessary for school leaders. We continually send messages to others, intentionally or otherwise. The manner in which we do so may be as important as the content of the message. Research demonstrates that we spend a majority of our time in schools communicating with "parents, members of the community, and other members of the organization" (Green, 2005, p. 86). Think for a moment about leaders you know who are good communicators. What makes them so effective, and what impact does their ability to communicate well have on the organization as a whole? Undoubtedly, you'll come up with several key reasons why enhancing communication is so vital to the proper functioning of your school as an organization. One of the primary goals we have as school leaders is to promote ongoing communication among faculty, staff, and with others among the faculty or with parents or other community representatives. Certainly, our ability to communicate determines the extent to which people understand and act upon our school vision.

Many books deal comprehensively with methods of good communication. The goal of this chapter is to begin to enable you to take your enhanced personal knowledge and your espoused theories and develop them into theories-in-use (Osterman & Kottkamp, 2004). Sharpening the interpersonal skills that are based on listening and communication skills is the first step that will facilitate that growth. You already may have experienced a sample of the kind of feedback that enhances communication in the process of writing your personal vision statement (see the volume on cultural leadership in this Principal Leadership Series or see Sullivan & Glanz, 2005). The descriptive feedback that you shared with your colleagues is representative of responses that foster communication. The second step is to develop the ability to make your wishes and needs known without putting the listener on the defensive. These strategies are called *assertion messages*.

As many of you have probably learned along life's road, we cannot control the other person's or group's response. We cannot *make* change happen. We can only learn and use strategies that encourage open interchange and subsequent problem solving.

> *"Communication is the lifeblood of the school."*
>
> —Fred C. Lunenburg and Allan C. Ornstein

This chapter will review some strategies and techniques for improving listening and communication skills. Much of this good work is drawn from my good friend and colleague Susan Sullivan, whom I've had the honor to work with on several projects (see, e.g., Sullivan & Glanz, 2005). The chapter also includes other suggestions for enhancing good communication verbally, in written fashion, and in social interactions. The important point here is that operational leadership is much more than organizing school files, setting up multicultural fairs, writing budget plans, and reading standard operations manuals. Operational leadership implies real action. Action inevitably occurs in our close work with people. Communication is our most valuable resource or method used to accomplish our objectives. Too often, we take good communication for granted, because we all communicate in some way. Yet, if one studies the topic, one realizes the skills necessary to communicate effectively. Leaders are successful or not mainly because of their ability or inability to communicate. Although this is important for any form of leadership, it is quite necessary for operational leaders.

What You Should Know About Communicating Effectively

- **Develop Listening Skills**—Practice an exercise to improve listening skills.
- **Communication Techniques**—Practice an exercise to enhance communication.
- **Avoid Barriers to Communication**—Learn to identify and avoid barriers to communication.

(Continued)

(Continued)

- **Using Assertion Messages**—Learn to use Bolton's (1986) assertion messages.
- **Keil's Six Essential Questions for Communicating for Results**—This section provides practical suggestions for principals drawn from the work of Keil (2005).
- **Simon and Newman's Five Suggestions for Enhancing Communication**—This section provides more commonsense suggestions for principals from Simon and Newman (2004).
- **Using E-mail**—Here are some simple suggestions for using and not using e-mail.
- **Running Effective Meetings**—Learn these simple guidelines for a common way we communicate.

1. DEVELOP LISTENING SKILLS

We are so busy that sometimes we don't listen. We have to make quick decisions every day, so we condition ourselves to react quickly. Sometimes such action may be premature. Listening first is critical to your effectiveness as a decision maker. How well do your superiors listen to you? Does their inattentiveness frustrate you? Now think about those you supervise, and try the following activity.

Turn to a neighbor. Each of you has one minute to respond to a series of simple questions about each other's professional life. Each of you talks for a minute. No one can take notes, and no questions or discussion is allowed. At the end of two minutes, each of you should recount to each other or to the whole group what you have learned about the colleague. As you try to recount the information your colleague shared, you may be amazed to see how little you remember and how inaccurate some of your recollections are. This exercise awakens the need to develop listening skills.

> *"Far too often, we equate communication with the ability to frame ideas and information in an interesting or persuasive manner. With the primary focus on the speaker, too little attention is paid to the listener."*
>
> —Karen Osterman and Robert Kottkamp

Table 6.1 Building a Community of Practice

Adult practice	
• College classroom	• Students describe where and what they teach and their past teaching experience, their reasons for taking the course, their professional aspirations.
• Leaders with other leaders	• Leaders talk about their leadership position and school and their goals, aspirations, and challenges.
• Professional development	• Staff explain, if appropriate, where and what they teach, the reason for choosing the workshop, and what they hope to learn and take back to their school or class.
• Group or team meeting	• Staff explain why they are participating, what role they would like to play, and what goals they see for the group.
• Parent meeting	• Parents or guardians describe who their child or children are, share something positive about their own or their children's experience in the school, and bring up a concern they would like addressed.
Student practice	
• K–12 classroom	• Students give their names, tell what class they were in and teacher(s) they had the previous year and what their favorite and most challenging subjects are. The students mention one thing they would like to learn this year.

SOURCE: Sullivan & Glanz, 2006, *Building Effective Learning Communities*, Corwin Press.

This activity can also be used with the school's leadership team or with staff, including school secretaries. Children of any age can also enhance their capacity to learn if they improve their listening skills. The suggestions in Table 6.1 are included to give you an idea of the types of questions that can be used at each level to increase participants' awareness of their listening skills.

Reflective Questions

1. What did you learn about yourself or the other person by doing this exercise?

2. Try this out in practice during the day. What have you remembered about the three parents you met today for the first time? Can you recall anything about them? Did you really listen to them?

3. Why are good listening skills so important for dealing with managerial functions as a principal?

---

2. COMMUNICATION TECHNIQUES

Awareness of how carefully we listen is the first step in improving our listening skills. The next step is to acquire techniques that will facilitate effective listening. Half of the battle is your ability to focus on the speaker; the other half is to communicate to the speaker that you are listening carefully and to verify that you have understood what the speaker is trying to express or convey.

The three types of techniques that follow promote effective listening and understanding (see Table 6.2).

- The techniques in the first category in Table 6.2, "Listening," have a dual purpose: They encourage the speaker to continue and indicate that you are following carefully; they support your listening by inserting brief comments that relate to the content of the message.
- The techniques in the second category, "Nonverbal cues," have similar effects: They clearly indicate to the speaker the listener's attention and free both the speaker and the listener from physical distractions and barriers that hinder interactions.
- The techniques in the third category, "Reflecting and clarifying," are the most important in terms of verifying understanding, and these are also the most frequently omitted. Most miscommunication results from the speaker saying one thing and the listener hearing another. How often do children say, "You aren't listening to me"?

Table 6.2   Communication Techniques

Listening	Nonverbal cues	Reflecting and clarifying
"Uh-huh"	Affirmative nods and smiles	"You're angry because . . ."
"OK"	Open body language (e.g., arms open)	"You feel . . . because . . ."
"I'm following you"	Appropriate distance from speaker—not too close or too far	"You seem quite upset."
"For instance"	Eye contact	
"And?"	Nondistracting environment	"So, you would like . . ."
		"I understand that you see the problem as . . ."
"Mmm"	Face speaker and lean forward	"I'm not sure, but I think you mean . . ."
"I understand"	Barrier-free space (e.g., desk not used as a blocker)	"I think you're saying . . ."
"This is great information for me"		
"Really?"		
"Then?"		
"So?"		
"Tell me more"		
"Go on"		
"I see"		
"Right"		

SOURCE: Sullivan & Glanz, 2006, *Building Effective Learning Communities*, Corwin Press.

Adults are often not as open, and they tend to hear from their own perspective without verifying. So many misunderstandings could be avoided through the use of these techniques. Now practice these three types of skills by pairing with a neighbor and have a conversation. Refer to the chart and see if you can appropriately use a particular communication technique.

Reflective Question

1. How was communication improved through the use of each of the three skills discussed on pages 96 and 97?

---

3. AVOID BARRIERS TO COMMUNICATION

You may be a better listener and know how to communicate, but you must also avoid certain barriers to communication. These barriers can have deleterious consequences for both the listener and the speaker. They discourage people from expressing themselves openly; they interrupt and often end the narration; they put the speaker on the defensive; and they prevent the listener from hearing the speaker's perspective. These barriers to communication are referred to as "spoilers" and high-risk responses, and as a general rule they should be avoided.

Three types of barriers are enumerated in Table 6.3. Read and study them and the examples provided. Then, engage in a mock conversation and have it audiotaped with permission of your partner. Play it back to first determine how well you communicated (see Table 6.2), and then see if you created, inadvertently, any of the barriers alluded to in Table 6.3.

Sullivan and Glanz (2006) explain that most of these barriers to communication are part of our theories-in-use and are ingrained in our language and habits. Ongoing practice is therefore vital to change.

4. USING ASSERTION MESSAGES

The focus thus far has been primarily on listening skills and the techniques that will encourage others to communicate. However, it is equally important to be able to express one's feelings and thoughts in a manner that transmits needs without putting the listener on the defensive. This type of communication is called an assertion message. One of the principal tenets of conflict resolution is the use of the "I" message instead of the accusatory "you" as each party explains his or her version of the events in question. Description from the "I" point of view is also a central principle of assertion messages.

Robert Bolton (1986), in *People Skills*, provides a comprehensive description of how to develop effective three-part assertion messages.

Table 6.3   Barriers to Communication*

Barrier type	Examples

1. Judging
   • Criticizing
   • Name calling and labeling
   • Diagnosing—analyzing motives instead of listening
   • Praising evaluatively
	1. Judging
	   • "You are lazy; your lesson plan is poor."
	   • "You are inexperienced, an intellectual."
	   • "You're taking out your anger on her."
	   • "I know what you need."
	   • "You're terrific!"

2. Solutions
   • Ordering
 	
   • Threatening
 	
   • Moralizing or preaching
   • Inappropriate questioning or prying
   • Advising
 	
   • Lecturing
	2. Solutions
	   • "You must . . ." "You have to . . ." "You will . . ."
	   • "If you don't . . ." "You had better or else."
	   • "It is your duty/responsibility; you should . . ."
	   • "Why?" "What?" "How?" "When?"
	
	   • "What I would do is . . ." "It would be best for you to . . ."
	   • "Here is why you are wrong . . ." "Do you realize . . .?"

3. Avoiding the other's concerns
   • Diverting
 	
   • Reassuring
 	
   • Withdrawing
 	
   • Sarcasm
	3. Avoiding the other's concerns
	
	   • "Speaking of . . ." "Apropos . . ." "You know what happened to . . .?"
	   • "It's not so bad . . ." "You're lucky . . ." "You'll feel better."
	   • "I'm very busy . . ." "I can't talk right now . . ." "I'll get back to you . . ."
	   • "I really feel sorry for you."

People Skills, by Robert Bolton (1986), is an excellent source of many communication skills.

SOURCE: Sullivan & Glanz, 2006, *Building Effective Learning Communities,* Corwin Press.

He states that assertion messages are the thinking being's response when one's space is violated as contrasted with the fight-or-flight response of our prehuman ancestors. We include verbal responses as well as actions in the behaviors that invade the asserter's personal space. Bolton refers to the goal of assertion messages as getting the other to change the behavior that is intruding on the asserter's territory. At the same time, he says that the message defends one's own turf without violating the other's space. The goal is for the recipient to devise a solution that maintains his or her own self-respect while meeting the asserter's needs. If we focus on the possibility of joint problem solving to produce a solution, it no longer is a win-lose situation but a win-win one. Bolton also cautions us not to use assertion messages in high-risk situations. His advice is that the situation should meet the following criteria:

1. There is a high probability that the other will alter the troublesome behavior.

2. There is a low probability that I will violate the other person's space.

3. There is little likelihood of diminishing the other person's self-esteem.

4. There is a low risk of damaging the relationship.

5. There is a low risk of diminishing motivation.

6. There is little likelihood that defensiveness will escalate to destructive levels.

Reflective Questions

1. Try to think of a situation where you felt someone intruded on your space and you did not assert yourself. What happened?

2. Think of a circumstance where you asserted yourself when you felt your space was violated. What happened?

3. What conclusions do you draw from your experiences?

The basic assertion message comprises three parts:

1. A nonjudgmental description of the behavior that is violating the asserter's space

2. An explanation of the asserter's feelings

3. A clarification of the concrete and tangible effect(s) of the other person's behavior on the asserter

The following examples will give you an idea of professional and personal situations where assertion can be effective (Ideas taken from Sullivan & Glanz, 2006, *Building Effective Learning Communities*, Corwin Press):

• You are the parent of a teenager who has been coming in late with his friends on weekends. They make a lot of noise, waking you up, and then you cannot fall back to sleep. You feel like getting up right then and saying, "How can you and your delinquent buddies be so inconsiderate? Any more noise and you're grounded for the rest of the weekend!" This response would combine three barriers in two sentences: judging ("delinquent buddies"), moralizing ("inconsiderate"), and threatening (grounding). Instead, you decide, after the most recent incident, to wait until the next evening after you both have had some rest, at which time you make the following assertion message:

1. Description: "When you come home late at night with your friends and make noise . . .
2. Feelings: "I get quite annoyed . . .
3. Effects: "because it wakes me up, I can't fall back to sleep, and then I'm tired the whole next day."

• A teacher in your school who shares a classroom with another teacher complains that when she returns from lunch, the chalkboard is always full of writing. She does not have enough time before the class begins to erase it well and put up her next class's information. She feels like saying, "It is every teacher's responsibility to clean up the classroom before the next teacher comes in. Please make sure that you erase the chalkboard before I return from lunch and prep." This response contains moralizing ("teacher's responsibility") and ordering ("make sure that you erase"). Therefore, she may decide to try the following message:

1. Description: "When I get back from prep or lunch and the board has writing on it . . .
2. Feelings: "I feel frustrated . . .
3. Effects: "because the class gets antsy while I erase it and try to get my information up."

• As principal, you are very orderly and well organized. Even in conversation, you like to finish your complete thought before letting the other person respond. You meet a fellow principal at a conference. This colleague is spontaneous and less structured than you. She always interjects her ideas before you get a chance to finish. It drives you crazy! You feel like saying, "Can't you control yourself? It's really rude to interrupt someone in the middle of a sentence." You know that that response is judgmental ("Can't you control yourself") and moralizing ("It's really rude"). So you decide to say:

1. Description: "When you interrupt me in the middle of a sentence or thought . . .
2. Feelings: "I feel irritated . . .
3. Effects: "because I lose track of my ideas and forget what I was saying."

A few final hints when using three-part assertion messages:

- Make sure your description of the behavior is specific.
- Be descriptive and objective—don't draw inferences or be judgmental.
- Be as brief as possible—concentrate on one behavior.
- Make sure that your assertion is not "displaced"—that you are not using a small issue instead of facing a bigger one, or ignoring small issues until they create a major issue.
- Don't take out your frustration with one person on another—yelling at your wife when you're angry with your boss (Bolton, 1986).

Reflective Question

1. How do Bolton's ideas help you communicate better? (See Sullivan & Glanz, 2006, for ways of practicing these assertion messages and other communication techniques.)

---

5. KEIL'S SIX ESSENTIAL QUESTIONS FOR COMMUNICATING FOR RESULTS

The importance of effective communication is axiomatic. No one would argue with the assertion that good principals are effective communicators. Yet this skill of communication is complex in that it entails much more than for a principal to be articulate and a dispenser of key information. In today's results-driven milieu, effective communication is more vital than ever for our success. Keil (2005) explains:

> There is a compelling need for principals to develop best practices in communication and to assess their own effectiveness so they can improve and sustain quality communication. To be understood—and to help constituents understand each other—principals must develop a systematic approach for assessing and benchmarking their communications. (p. 28)

Is the Right Person Communicating?

Communication occurs all the time by everyone. You are not the sole communicator, nor can you control all the information about your school. You can, however, according to Keil (2005), improve the effectiveness of communication in the following three ways:

- "Identifying the sources of information that are perceived as credible"—Rumors, for instance, abound in all organizations. Let's say a rumor circulates that the superintendent is intending to reassign your current assistant principal. Before jumping to conclusions or even accepting this information as accurate, you should ask yourself, "From where is this information originating?" If it comes from a disgruntled teacher under the supervision of your AP, you may conclude one thing. If it comes from your trusted secretary who just received a call from the central office, you might take a different stance (e.g., to inquire further).

- "Involving competent people in the communication process"—As principal, you should remain aware of people you can or cannot trust for communicating information accurately. Teachers, for instance, should be kept informed of key information from the central office pertaining to curricular matters. Who delivers such information, and under what circumstances, should not be taken for granted.

- "Clearly defining the aims and purposes of the communication"—Before you rush out to communicate some information about someone or any matter, make certain you fully understand why you are communicating the information and what consequence it may have on those receiving it.

Keil (2005) sums up by explaining, "By focusing on these three actions, principals can determine whether the person speaking is reliable, acceptable, and considered credible by those for whom the message is intended" (p. 29).

Is the Information Valuable and Meaningful?

Communication for communication's sake is not a good enough rationale for delivering information. Why is it necessary to dispense this information, and why at this particular time? What are the consequences for the organization or certain individuals if this information should be conveyed inaccurately or prematurely? Some suggestions for ensuring accurate information include verifying that the communication is "clear and coherent," that the language used is "familiar to and understood by the intended audience," and that not too much information is "shared at any one time" (Keil, 2005, p. 29).

Do the Constituents Feel Informed?

"We're the last to find out," complained a group of teachers in the teachers' cafeteria. Upset to hear that Teacher's Choice funds were going to be cut in half, teachers were irritated not necessarily because of the diminished funds but more likely as a result of not being informed by the principal in a timely and respectful manner. Keil (2005) stresses, "It is important for people in the school community to feel informed." She continues, "Principals must pay attention to the importance of active involvement in the communication processes and establish open channels of communication for everyone" (p. 29). I recall a school administrator who received many complaints because he did not communicate the criteria he used to award special funds to teachers for classroom supplies. Teachers had to apply for the district funds by writing a description of how they would use such funds to promote pupil learning. Funds were distributed to selected teachers "without communicating the standards by which these decisions were made," claimed one teacher. Certainly, we have difficult decisions to make, but we must remain savvy enough to keep lines of communication open in order to inform all our constituents of relevant information. Keil offers these suggestions for developing a system of effective communication:

• "Establish an open communication policy that is understood by everyone." A written Policy and Procedures Manual is helpful.

• "Create lines of communication that are as short and direct as possible for staff members, students, parents, and other constituencies." Use of directed memoranda, PA announcements, monthly newsletter, e-mails, and Web page information are some useful methods.

Your effectiveness as a leader and manager will be measured by the manner and extent to which you keep your constituents informed.

Am I Listening to Concerns?

In the discussion summarized earlier in the chapter, Keil (2005) shrewdly observes, "All principals have their share of problems, complainers, and naysayers, but recognizing the importance of listening to those who should be heard . . . helps build good relationships and a climate of trust" (p. 30). "Nah, she never really listens to us" or "He says he hears our concerns, but he does nothing about them" are complaints some teachers may make about their principals. Communication is affirmed by our actions, not merely by our words. We may demonstrate that we care by providing opportunities for teachers and others to share their concerns. We may have an open-door policy or we may speak with teachers during morning lineups, at lunchtime, or at dismissal. Being available is important, as is affirming what you hear by nodding or paraphrasing what the person has stated. The true test of communication, however, is taking some action. Such action might not always be in favor of a teacher complaint, for instance. Still, you should convey your decision to the relevant parties in a prompt, clear, decisive, and respectful manner.

Is Communication Ongoing and Systematic?

Establishing methods or networks of communication is essential. Here are some ways you may do so:

- Post relevant information on the bulletin board in the main office. Everyone will know that's the place to look for key information. Therefore, make sure you post important information for teachers (e.g., district office job opportunities, instructional or curricular announcements).
- Publish a weekly Monday morning newsletter. The newsletter can be brief, even one back-to-back page of useful announcements, updates, and so forth.
- Update the school Web page weekly.
- Send relevant e-mails to teachers.

The success of your communication system can be attested to by comments such as these:

- "Yes, we receive announcements about matters that concern us in a timely manner and at regular intervals throughout the school year."
- "Sure, whenever I want to know what's happening, I check out the 'What's Happening' section of our school's Web page."
- "My principal keeps me informed because he's always out there, in the hallways, school yard, teacher's cafeteria, all over speaking to us and keeping us informed."
- "E-mails . . . sometimes we get too many, but no one can say we're not informed."

Reflective Question

1. Which of Keil's ideas make the most practical sense to you? Explain and give examples how you might use them.

---

6. SIMON AND NEWMAN'S FIVE SUGGESTIONS FOR ENHANCING COMMUNICATION

"The ability to effectively communicate with all school community members can mean the difference between an average principal and one who is very effective" (Simon & Newman, 2004, p. 27). Simon and Newman offer several easy-to-implement suggestions for enhancing your communicative abilities:

Suggestion 1: How to Use the Telephone

Communicating by telephone is an invaluable means of giving someone your undivided attention and dealing with urgent matters. Although e-mail is a quick and easy way of communicating, when it comes to more detailed and serious issues, telephone conversations are more advisable. Such communications tend to lead to fewer misinterpretations, and talking by telephone gives the receiver the feeling that you are devoting your time to address her or his concern. Making people feel special and listened to will go a long way to building and maintaining positive relationships within the school community.

Suggestion 2: Visibility—Leading by Walking Around

We are bombarded by so much paperwork, more today than ever. We may feel pressured to remain in our offices to complete the paperwork and reports that are due in a short time. Fight against that pressure. Plan to get out of your office. Schedule time to visit classrooms, tour the building and grounds, observe a teacher, conduct a demonstration lesson, and so on. As you are about the school, feel free to schmooze and shoot the breeze with your staff. Developing and solidifying interpersonal relationships is accomplished through such activities. Teachers, students, parents, and staff want to see you. You have a great chance to communicate some of the latest information through these informal chats.

Suggestion 3: The Working Lunch

You might be inclined to eat alone. Get out and eat with the staff. Visit the cafeteria regularly. "When possible," Simon and Newman (2004) suggest,

use district money to provide pizza or sandwiches for small informal group meetings with you. . . . These lunches should not be formal affairs; rather, they should be opportunities for the members of the school community to have a casual meet-ing with the principal in his or her office. (p. 29)

Suggestion 4: Parents as Partners

Don't ignore your students' parents. Use these forums to com-municate with them:

1. E-mail

2. Memoranda

3. Formal and informal meetings

4. Web page info

Suggestion 5: Public Presentations

You enjoy speaking. Get out there and speak to a local Rotary group, a parents' association, a local conference, at a local college, and so forth. Use these speaking engagements to reinforce your school's mission, for instance, or use the opportunity to engage the audience on some hot educational topic in the news.

Reflective Question

1. Which of Simon and Newman's ideas make the most practical sense to you? Explain and give examples of how you might use them.

---

7. USING E-MAIL

Communication today is frequently conducted via e-mail. It's quick, convenient, and fast. Often, someone will write something in an e-mail that they wouldn't dare say face to face with the person. Psychologically, the sender feels more comfortable. Yet, the receiver may not appreciate the comment and may harbor resentment. Added to this feeling is the fact that the receiver now has written proof of the comment. Some people like e-mail communication because they can literally control the conversation. Some people prefer e-mail communication for that reason alone. Although there are many advantages of e-mail, there are some additional caveats you should be concerned about. First, you should realize that it is virtually impossible for you to retract an e-mail message once you've hit the "send" key. So be careful—read and reread your e-mail message to make certain that it expresses precisely what you want to say. Take the position of the recipient. How will he or she interpret your message? Don't forget that subtleties of voice inflection, accents, and body language are absent in e-mail communications. Misinterpretations are very common. Also, know that whatever you write in an e-mail can be read by anyone. Most servers are not completely secure. So, whenever you write something, think about this notion: If I don't want this to be read by everyone, then I shouldn't send it. For instance, if you intend to send an e-mail that may disparage someone, assume that someone will find out. Therefore, you may want to think twice about sending that e-mail message.

Alvy and Robbins's (1998, pp. 104–105) eight suggestions for using e-mail effectively are also helpful:

- Keep messages short, and ask colleagues to do the same.
- Do not feel compelled to read each message. Make a decision to read or delete messages after reading the headings.
- Have the secretary scan e-mail messages to delete unimportant ones.
- Try to read and respond to e-mail messages in one sitting. Do not worry if not all messages are reviewed. Critical correspondence should not be sent via e-mail.
- Promote schoolwide electronic bulletin boards for selected topics so that each topic does not appear on everyone's system.
- Do not use e-mail as a substitute for important one-to-one or group interactions.
- Avoid using e-mail for confidential and sensitive topics. Security systems break down, and information can be misused.
- Your e-mail address is as important as your phone number, so distribute it cautiously.

E-mail communication has its benefits and disadvantages. Used as the sole or main form of communication, e-mail can present major problems. Used thoughtfully and sparingly, it can be an effective means of conveying information.

Reflective Question

1. Can you relate a positive and a not-so-positive experience you've had with e-mail communication?

---

8. RUNNING EFFECTIVE MEETINGS

We cannot cover every aspect of effective communication in this chapter. But several key ideas have been highlighted. This last idea or best practice entails brief suggestions for communicating via meetings, which are common in our business. We conduct meetings all the time, and such opportunities are excellent venues for sharing information and exchanging ideas. Here are some brief, commonsense guidelines that may serve to remind you of what's important:

- Develop a purpose. A meeting should have a goal and a series of clear objectives.

- Draft an agenda. Sequence topics to be discussed.

- Prepare handouts and materials. Plan and prepare everything in advance.

- Review agenda with an experienced AP or principal. Solicit input and suggestions from others.

- Keep to the agenda when conducting the meeting.

- Solicit input from all participants.

- Monitor self-talk. Don't dominate conversations.

- Purchase the best small book on the subject: *Energize Your Meetings With Laughter* by Sheila Feigelson (1998). Contents include: Chapter 1. Making Room for Laughter; Chapter 2. Four Major Types

of Meetings; Chapter 3. Announcing Your Meeting With Flair;
Chapter 4. Arrivals and First Impressions; Chapter 5. Look Who's
Here! Introducing Participants; Chapter 6. As the Meeting Moves:
Print, Props, and Visual Aids; Chapter 7. Dividing Into Smaller
Groups; Chapter 8. Fun With Food; Chapter 9. Breaks That
Invigorate; Chapter 10. Ending the Meeting on a Positive Note;
Chapter 11. The Power of Saying Thanks; Chapter 12. Inviting
Laughter to Your Next Meeting; and a Resources section.

Reflective Question

1. How can running an effective meeting enhance communication
   in your school?

CONCLUSION

Communication is at once obvious yet complex. You speak
words, people hear them, and they may even nod their heads in
affirmation. Then, to your surprise, they act in ways that indicate they didn't follow your advice. "Did they misinterpret what
I said?" you may ask, "or did they intentionally not follow my
directives?" The other person might respond, "Well, I didn't
think you were 'directing' me, only suggesting what I might do."
I am certain we have all experienced similar miscommunications. Miscommunication is anathema to a school administrator. Standard operational procedures are jeopardized, confusion
results, and chaos prevails.

In this chapter, several ideas about improving communications were presented along with some practice exercises. Mindful
and serious attention to these matters is suggested. Whether you
communicate in person, via e-mail, with memoranda, through
meetings, or by any other form or combination of ways of communicating, you should realize that your success as a leader
requires effective communication. Basic procedures for running a
school cannot be fully in place without a systematic and consistent communications network. Methods for dispelling rumors, for

instance, should be developed. As principal, you must always be aware of miscommunications and take steps to ensure that these muddled communications are cleared up. You should ensure that all parties have access to relevant information and that steps are taken to make sure that information is provided in a variety of ways. The complexities of the social organization we live in require that we attend to these matters.

CHAPTER SEVEN

Best Practices in Personal Management

"All principals, regardless of experience, level of school, size of school, type of school district . . . have very important, difficult, and demanding jobs."

—John C. Daresh

"Principals must take care of themselves in order to care for others."

—Pam Robbins and Harvey B. Alvy

"Leaders know themselves; they know their strengths and nurture them."

—Warren Bennis

I f management is essentially about taking care of things, then a book on this topic should have something to offer on personal management. Without attention to one's self, management of anything else would be difficult, to say the least. This final chapter of the book, then, addresses some practical approaches and suggestions for managing your personal affairs so that you can indeed help others.

What You Should Know About Personal Management

- **Dealing With Stress**—Suggestions for handling stress are discussed.
- **Striving for Personal Renewal**—A variety of suggestions for addressing personal renewal are offered.

---

1. DEALING WITH STRESS

Stress is a reality that you deal with on a daily basis. Although the term *stress* has a negative connotation, you should be aware of three kinds of stress:

- Distress (negative stress—such as worry, anxiety, fear, disappointment, hatred, and overload)
- Stress (neutral stress—such as change, noise, money, expectations, and people)
- Eustress (positive stress—such as tenure, promotion, love, vacation, and success)

I define *stress* as a demand on our being—physical, emotional, or mental—that exceeds our ability to cope. Both neutral and positive stress can quickly turn into distress if uncontrolled. All three kinds of stress, however, may produce similar negative feelings in us. In that sense, stress is stress. Keep in mind the following points:

- Stress is inevitable. As long as you are alive, stress will occur.
- Accept stress for what it is. See stress as an opportunity to reach your potential.
- Nothing in life that is worthwhile comes easy.
- Don't give up.

> *There is an apocryphal tale of a farmer who owned the only horse in town. One night, the horse broke loose and people asked him, "Isn't that terrible?"*
>
> *He answered, "Perhaps."*
> *The next day, the horse returned with wild mares following him. "Isn't that wonderful?" they asked.*
> *"Perhaps."*
> *Two days later, the farmer's son fell off one of the wild horses and fractured his leg.*
> *"Isn't that terrible?"*
> *"Perhaps."*
> *A week later, the army recruiters came to town and drafted all the young men of the area, except for the farmer's son, because of his broken leg.*

We all have setbacks. Frequently they are disguised blessings. Perhaps you can think about situations that arose on the job that at first appeared horrible but that later turned out to be somewhat positive.

Four Ways to Relieve Stress

I have used the following four approaches with some of my principal colleagues who had difficulty in dealing with the stress associated with their work on the job.

- Cognitive sophistication
- Positive affirmations
- Developing networks of support
- Humor

1. Cognitive Sophistication (Framing the Proper Attitude)

Lifestyle and attitude play an enormous role in relieving stress and enhancing general well-being. Books have been written on these topics, and I recommend you visit the "self-help" section of your local bookstore, or you may wish to read my own contribution to the subject (Glanz, 2000).

Here, I want to present an eight-step approach for dealing with any stressor or problem that you may confront. This approach to attitude development involves an idea known as cognitive sophistication; that is, confronting a stressful situation by verbally challenging the logic of its consequences. Below are eight steps I have developed that have helped me and my students. I'll then provide one example of how I use them. Then it's up to you to practice the steps and see how they work for you.

Step 1: Acknowledge Your Problem or Stressor (Consciousness)

Sit down in a quiet place and verbalize the problem to yourself (e.g., "I can't handle the seemingly endless complaints of this job"). In this step, you state the problem clearly and forthrightly. This approach demonstrates that you are aware of the problem. You'd be surprised how often we really aren't aware of what is causing our tension.

Although I'll later ask you to go through these eight steps, consider this first step: What is bothering you—what is causing you stress? Verbalize the problem.

Step 2: Affirm Your Feelings (Emotional)

State how you feel about the situation (e.g., "Whenever I'm confronted with another complaint about our technology lab, I want to scream"). Stress can wreak havoc on our emotions. We often conceal how we feel, and thus more tension builds. In our culture, men, especially, do not express their emotions. This step encourages you to express how you feel, at least to yourself, if not to a confidant.

Step 3: Control Your Reaction (Intellect)

Now that you are conscious of the problem and have expressed how you feel about it, you must now gain control over it intellectually by affirming ownership over the problem and acknowledging your ability to deal with it.

Police officers are sometimes verbally abused, as are educators, by their clients, if you will. Such behavior is reprehensible. But do police officers have the right to confront such abuse by taking out their gun and shooting the person? Of course not. They are trained to remain stoic in such situations; they are, after all, professionals. They, like us educators, must realize their obligations to remain professional under all circumstances. In other words, they must control their reactions to the situation. One way of doing so would be to ask, "What will happen if I take this gun out and shoot this person? What will be the consequences of my actions?" Those individuals who are overcome by their emotions do not address these questions. This step encourages you to control your reaction to the problem (e.g., "It's my problem. I will control my reaction. I realize the consequences of my actions. I take responsibility."). What have you done in the past to lose control? How can you in the future control your reaction?

Step 4: Consider Your Options

At this stage, you should consider what alternatives you have for dealing with the problem. You may, for example, do nothing and accept the situation. You may discuss the problem with someone. You may be able to do a number of things. Ask yourself at this step, "What are the options for dealing with my problem?" You will realize that *several* options exist. Whether or not you wish to pursue any of them is another matter. Options do exist. What are *your* options?

Step 5: Breathe and Relax

As you consider your options, simultaneously practice a breathing exercise or two. Simply take some deep breaths in and out. These exercises will allow you to clear your mind and enable you to better confront your problem.

Step 6: Reconsider Consequences

You still, at this stage, have not done anything. Consider your options again and their consequences. Be deliberate and patient in your thinking.

Step 7: Act

Now it's time to act. Do something, *or* decide not to act (e.g., "I'll ignore the complaints and hope people just wanted to let off steam"). Whatever you decide, you'll feel empowered, in control. Realize that whatever you now decide is not irrevocable (see the next step).

Step 8: Reconsider, Act, Reconsider, Act

Once you've decided on a course of action and some time has passed, you can now reconsider your options. You may decide that a new course of action is in order. The process I've described is cyclical. Apply these steps again and again as necessary.

Applying the Eight Steps: "I can't seem to find the time for instructional leadership when I seem to go from one management crisis to another. I keep putting out fire after fire. I'm overwhelmed; it never seems to stop. I have no help here. I feel angry and upset with myself. It is my responsibility to get things done as principal. I know I have the ability to handle this. I can make the time for what's really important. I need to realize that I shouldn't fret over things I can't control and focus on things I can. Now, what are my options? I can carve out special time on my calendar to supervise my teachers. I could delegate authority more to my competent APs and get over the feeling that I have to do it all myself. Let me consider what I will do, but first I'll practice some breathing exercises. Let me now consider my options again and the consequences of each. Okay, I will now prioritize my responsibilities. At a later date, I can reconsider my decision."

2. Positive Affirmations and Thoughts

As educators, we are bound by our perspectives, our unique vantage points. Reality is perceived and understood through the perspective of our belief systems, which are in turn based on assumptions gleaned from our experiences. Reality is dependent on our thinking patterns, belief systems, and mind-sets. Our belief systems are intimately connected to the language we use to articulate and communicate meanings that influence our actions and behaviors. How we think shapes the world in which we live. As Arthur Schopenhauer, German philosopher, once posited, "The world in which a man lives shapes itself chiefly by the way in which he looks at it."

How do you look at the world? What do you believe? Do you believe that your thoughts can influence not only how you look at things but how you feel? Belief that your thoughts can deeply affect you is essential to controlling stress.

"I think I can, I think I can . . . I know I can."

"They can do all because they think they can."
(Virgil, *Aeneid*, 19 BC)

Research on the use of positive affirmations indicates that positive thinking can have a powerful influence on how you react to stress. Try repeating several phrases in an almost mantra-like fashion. (Hint: I have found it very helpful to write my affirmation on a small index card. I keep it with me throughout the day and repeat the affirmation as needed.) This practice can condition your thought patterns in ways you wouldn't imagine. Try each of these affirmations over the course of the next week. What effect do they have on helping you relieve stress associated with your job?

- "I can succeed as principal."
- "Others before me did, why can't I?"
- "I can influence the way I feel."
- "I will not feel as if I have to meet everyone's expectations."
- "I will not run away from a problem. I will resolve the problem."
- "Take one step at a time, and don't get overwhelmed."
- "It's OK to fail, to make a mistake."
- "I am responsible for my actions and reactions."
- "I think and know I can."
- "I will find time for what I consider most important."

3. Building Strong Professional and Personal Networks of Support

Finding an individual or individuals who can commiserate with your plight is very effective in allaying your apprehensions. Having someone you can speak to goes a long way toward helping you release your anxieties. For instance, as one former student aptly put it, "Who else can I talk to? Who else will work this through with me? I find that talking to my spouse really helps. I have also found a colleague in class who shares my feelings. Together we'll make this work." Other ways to build strong professional and personal support mechanisms can help relieve stress:

- Venting to other colleagues (i.e., principals)
- Joining a Rotary club or civic association
- Seeking assistance from someone who is currently experiencing what you are
- Sustaining yourself by developing strong friendship bonds (inside and outside the workplace)
- Attending professional association conferences and attending meetings
- Partaking in blog sessions

4. Humor

Evidence clearly demonstrates that humor or laughter can decrease anxiety and stress, improve self-esteem, and increase motivation and perceived quality of life. You must read (or reread) Norman Cousins's *Anatomy of an Illness*, which tells the moving story of his successful fight against a crippling disease and demonstrates what the mind and body working together can do to overcome illness. The power of laughter and humor is emphasized.

What happens if you don't feel like laughing or you consider yourself not to be a very "humorous" person? Rent videos of your favorite funny movies or comedians. Watching the skits of the Marx Brothers, Abbott and Costello, or whomever for hours can relieve stress much more than you may realize. Try it today; visit a video store that carries these "old-time movies." Don't like video stores? Share humorous anecdotes or situations with a spouse or colleague.

I also suggest that you skip the 10:00 or 11:00 nightly news and watch instead Jay Leno's "Headlines" or read a good book, for example. Falling asleep with "happy" thoughts is more conducive to establishing a relaxed frame of mind. You'll sleep much better and awake energized.

Simon and Newman (2004) offer some rather simple suggestions for dealing with the stress that is so much a part of our day:

- Keep a journal.
- Attend conferences.
- Join a study group.
- Keep a portfolio of career accomplishments.
- Prepare future principals.
- Attend administrative retreats.

- Pamper yourself.
- Keep reading and sharing.

Reflective Questions

1. Which of these suggestions make the most sense for you?

2. What other strategies can you identify to reduce stress?

---

2. STRIVING FOR PERSONAL RENEWAL

Personal renewal refers to much more than just relieving stress. It refers to a full gamut of personal strategies aimed at keeping your interests and energy alive. From time to time, we all feel burned out a bit. We need to take a break. We need to take time to reflect and find ways of rekindling that spark that lies deep within. Effective operational leaders, by the way, realize that teachers also need such rejuvenation. The following ideas are aimed to suggest ways of achieving personal management or control over our destinies. Doing so will reinvigorate us and allow us to achieve our potential as educational leaders. You can't help anyone else without first taking care of yourself.

Young (2004) has his own tips for personal management that he calls plainly and to the point "taking care of yourself." His practical suggestions include the following:

- "Keep fit": "Principals who are physically fit tire less easily after long days, appear happier, and suffer less from depression" (p. 162).

- "Don't smoke": Young gets to the heart of the matter. First of all, he says, "Smokers smell." Second, you could die. "The principalship is demanding. It requires a strong person to persevere. Think about this," he says. "Lengthen your life. Increase the confidence and trust of the school board members who place their children in your care. Do you want to be a person with good health habits or a smoker with potential medical bills and a shorter life span?" (p. 163).

- "Develop a winning attitude" (p. 164). Maintaining a positive outlook despite the travails we encounter is so important. People with positive dispositions know they will succeed with hard work.

- "Arrive early, go home early. Even if you take work home": He continues, "Structure your day and allow time for you. Avoid burnout. Exercise, visit friends, volunteer at a nursing home, read, shop, do something that helps draw you away from the paperwork activities that have accumulated throughout the day. Remember to delegate" (pp. 165–166).

Young (2004) ends his practical suggestions in no less dramatic fashion by admonishing us with a sober thought:

> When you retire, or worse, lie on your deathbed, it is highly unlikely that you will wish that you had spent even more hours in the office after work. Enjoy a hobby. Get another life. Take care of yourself. (p. 166)

Daresh (2001) acknowledges the importance of attending to your personal needs. He suggests the following strategies:

- "Find a mentor" (p. 126): Find someone whom you respect and who is a good listener. This person should also have a positive disposition. The person should be a creative problem solver, not someone who merely listens.

- "Develop networks" (p. 128): Get out there and learn from others. Share thoughts and problems with principal colleagues at central office meetings, at local conferences, via e-mail correspondences, and through Listservs and blogs.

- "Participate in professional associations" (p. 129): At least twice a year, attend some sort of national conference (e.g., that of the National Association of Secondary School Principals or the Association for Supervision and Curriculum Development). Meeting and speaking with colleagues across the country, if not the world, will comfort you and bring you many ideas.

- "Maintain personal and family support" (p. 130): Do not miss your annual checkup. Make certain you exercise. Don't say, "Well, I run around all day." That's not exercise, that's "running around in a frenzied, harried state." Get out into the fresh air. Learn a new sport or physical activity (e.g., martial arts, yoga, dancing). Spend time alone reading a novel or other good book. Read research studies and books in your field of specialization. The ideas you gain might be invaluable.

Young (2004, pp. 168–184) mentions Daresh's (2001) suggestions and adds the following:

- "Avoid the status quo syndrome." Think creatively. Surround yourself with exciting people who challenge you. Find ways of doing things differently.

- "Keep your portfolio and résumé current." Maintain a portfolio of all your work and accomplishments. Save congratulatory letters and e-mails. Putting together such a portfolio is fun, and in times of crisis it will remind you how valued you truly are to your organization.

- "Write." Consider writing a small article for a local, state, or national journal. Even consider writing a book on your experiences. Ask yourself, "What do I have to say that others might find useful?" Start by writing for a local newspaper.

- "Improve your speaking skills." Take a course, or simply get out there to Rotary clubs and conferences and share your experiences and ideas for improving our schools. Speak to parent groups and other community members. Form reading groups with follow-up discussions.

- "Give professional presentations." When you attend national conferences, you'll see many of your colleagues delivering papers on a variety of topics. Consider doing likewise. Perhaps you could team up with a professor from a local college or university. They will generally welcome your participation on a research project that will eventuate in an article or presentation.

- "Invest in professional attire." Take care of yourself; look good. If you haven't bought some new outfits in recent years, do so. Besides the effect it'll have on others, you'll feel good about yourself, renewed. It's simply human nature to feel that way.

- "Join your state and national professional associations." Are you a member of these associations? If not, become a member of three or four such organizations. You'll receive their newsletter, correspondences, or journals.

Other recommendations include the following:

- Decide to get your doctorate. You have a master's degree already. Going for the doctorate, however, will be a big leap forward. You will be invigorated by new ideas and views of your professors. You'll likely read the works of the top scholars in your field. You'll be able to select a research topic of your interest to become expert in. The sense of renewal and accomplishment you'll gain from this achievement will be immeasurable.

- Take a day for self-renewal. I'm not a great fan of vacations. Sure, I enjoy a getaway like everyone else, but sometimes I need a vacation from the vacation, if you know what I mean. What really works for me is taking a "health day" every so often. I try to plan this on a day when not too much is going on. I'll usually stay home and "chill out." I may read a good book in my recreation room, take in a movie, rent a video, exercise, take in a play, or do anything that relaxes me. These "health" days are great, because I feel invigorated and even eager to return the next day fully energized. I find I can accomplish much more in a week in which I took off that day than if I hadn't.

Reflective Question

1. What other suggestions can you make to achieve self-renewal?

CONCLUSION

When I conceived of and wrote this chapter, I had no idea there was a field of specialization known as "personal management." There are personal management consultants, books, seminars, and much more. Do as I did, visit www.google.com and type in "personal management." You'll discover a plethora of resources and ideas that can extend your understanding of and work toward your own management. The important point here is worth repeating. As principal, you are responsible for managing others, indeed your entire school. My father once said that he saw so many people who preached to others without following their own advice. It's like the saying that goes "the shoemaker's kids often go without shoes." How can you manage others when you are falling apart? I once heard a talk show host who was usually rude speaking rather empathetically to a caller who lamented that he was going through "rough times." The caller explained that he was gaining weight, he couldn't sleep well, he was on various medications for recent health issues, his teenage son had just been arrested for smoking marijuana, and his wife had just left him. "I don't know what to do with myself. I have no direction in my life. I am at my wits' end," reported the caller. The talk show host tried to offer some keen advice. Then, the host asked, "By the way, what do you do for a living?" The man replied, "I'm a school guidance counselor!"

Taking care of yourself physically, emotionally, and intellectually is imperative. If you need assistance, seek help from a personal trainer or mentor. Our success in work depends a great deal on the extent to which we personally manage our own life and situations. Good luck.

Conclusion

Making Operational Leadership a Reality

This book has underscored the importance of school management. If you do not attend to operational leadership, you will falter in other leadership enterprises. Attending to the foundational aspects of management is therefore imperative. This book has lighted various, not all, management issues and tasks that are part of your responsibility as principal. The real challenge, however, is to balance management imperatives with leadership opportunities. Perhaps the way to achieve such a balance is not to conceive of management and leadership as two separate entities but rather "as a combined conceptualized role of the principal. . . . Surely certain tasks will tend to be more managerial than leadership, but the principal's role should be conceptualized as one in which both leadership and management are important" (Matthews & Crow, 2003, p. 177).

Some final suggestions for making this balance between management and leadership a reality include the following ideas, among others:

- Assess your ability to manage a school and your belief that leading your school is most imperative.

- Affirm that both leadership and management are essential and must be attended to daily in order to achieve success as a principal.

- Envision in both theory and practice that management and leadership are two sides of one coin and that you should therefore utilize your management skills to further leadership goals.

- Affirm the preceding vision by "supporting" leadership initiatives through "management efforts" that include money, personnel, time, and information (Matthews & Crow, 2003, p. 177).
  a. "Money" (p. 177): Attend to budgetary issues to support reform initiatives such as instructional improvement projects.
  b. "Personnel" (p. 179): Providing for and organizing workshops or professional development programs for all school personnel is necessary to support cultural, instructional, and strategic leadership.
  c. "Time" (p. 180): Attend to time management through intelligent and considerate scheduling, whether it's planning to free teachers to attend workshops or to provide for common prep periods so that groups of teachers may form leadership committees.
  d. "Information" (p. 180): Whether it's collecting information via the Internet to support the new schoolwide Balanced Literacy program to teach reading to fourth graders or incorporating data-driven decision making to inform classroom practice, you need to manage information in an efficient and organized manner.

- Furthermore, affirm the combination of management and leadership by attending to "planning" initiatives (Matthews & Crow, 2003, p. 182). Managing a strategic planning initiative is a tedious, yet important, responsibility as principal. Good management skills are required for short- and long-range planning (see Principal Leadership Series volume on strategic planning).

- You can also affirm the combination of management and leadership by "taking action" (Matthews & Crow, 2003, p. 184). There's a cute riddle or story I once heard: Three frogs are sitting on a log. Two decided to jump off. So how many are left? Answer: Three, because deciding to do something and actually doing so are two different things. We can plan to carry out our initiatives, but eventually we must actually implement them. Only someone who is well organized, makes efficient use of time, schedules appropriately, handles budgetary issues, attends to human resource exigencies, and fosters good communication will be able to take appropriate actions to move the school forward.

- Finally, management and leadership come together when you evaluate and assess your efforts. Good management skills are necessary for data collection, analysis, and interpretation. Assessment results can then be used to improve instruction in classrooms and schoolwide.

Matthews and Crow's (2003) comments are a fitting conclusion to this book that focuses on principal as manager:

> The role of the principal as manager is key in the daily planning, organizing, operating, executing, budgeting, maintaining, and scheduling of numerous processes, activities, and tasks that permit a school to accomplish its goals as a learning community. (p. 192)

Resource A

Realities of Operational Leadership:
In-Basket Simulations

This section highlights some of the realities of operational leadership using an approach called "In-Basket Simulations." It is a study technique derived from an approach used when I studied for licensure as a principal in New York City. The approach was developed by the Institute for Research and Professional Development (http://www.nycenet.edu/opm/opm/profservices/rfp1b723.html). Scenarios that you as a principal might encounter are presented for your reaction. For instance, "A letter from an irate parent complaining that her child is intentionally being ignored during instruction in class by the teacher is sent to your attention. What would you do?" Challenging you to confront real-life phenomena under controlled conditions, these simulated in-basket items will prompt critical inquiry.

Here are suggestions to guide you as you complete these in-basket exercises:

1. Think and respond as if you are a principal, not a teacher or an assistant principal.

2. Place yourself mentally in each situation as if the case were actually happening to you.

3. Draw on your experiences and from what you've learned from others. Think of a principal you respect, and ask yourself, "What would Mr. or Ms. X have done?"

4. Make distinctions between actions you would personally take and actions you would delegate to others.

5. Utilize resources (personnel or otherwise) to assist you.

6. Think about your response, and then share it with a colleague for her or his reaction.

7. Record your response, and then a day later reread the scenario and your response. Would you still have reacted the same way?

During an interview, you are asked to respond to the following scenarios:

• You are a newly appointed principal to an intermediate school in which the former principal never considered management-related problems or issues. She either ignored them or delegated them to others without checking on them. You feel the school is consequently "falling apart" because of her lack of attention to managerial responsibilities. What are the first steps you'd take?

• Your superintendent informs you that several parents have registered formal complaints that the physical plant of your school is deteriorating under your watch. Bathrooms, they complain, are rarely cleaned promptly, and lightbulbs are rarely replaced in dark corners of the building. How do you respond?

• You are a new principal of a fairly large school. You find yourself involved in day-to-day school management and operational issues, but you can't seem to find time for your true interest and love, instructional improvement. How do you balance the two responsibilities?

• The IEP team needs your assistance, because they say they are meeting resistance from several teachers for including students with disabilities in their classrooms. You are cognizant of your role as principal to identify and refer students who might have a disability. You also affirm your role in due process for them and take part on the IEP team. You also know you must serve as a facilitator to help teachers accept these children in their classes. How would you go about doing so? Explain the management strategies you might employ.

• You want to establish Collaborative Team Teaching (CTT) classes, but your faculty are resisting the idea. How would you go about staffing the CTT program? Describe how you would go about recruiting and selecting new faculty for your school.

• A teacher complains that she is being sexually harassed by a new teacher, Mr. Smith. What do you do?

• Your school has instituted a new Balanced Literacy program and the Workshop Model of instruction for all grades. You must incorporate block scheduling to facilitate such instructional efforts. How might you go about doing so, given you have never block-scheduled before?

• Mr. Schulenberg, the music chair, informs you that he needs a few new musical instruments, because several instruments have recently been damaged because of poor storage procedures. Not included in the annual budget that he submitted to you, these musical instruments are necessary in order for Mr. Schulenberg to prepare for the forthcoming schoolwide Music Fair at the high school. How do you rearrange the budget to accommodate his request?

• You've been informed by the central office that your instructional budget will be cut in half for the next academic year. You know you have planned for several instructional initiatives that require additional funding. What do you do?

• How do you use technology as a management tool?

• What are some ways you can raise money for your school?

• A reporter from Channel 7 calls you to ask if she can come to your school tomorrow to interview students on school and neighborhood violence. What do you say?

• The gifted program in your school has been in effect for five years without ever having gone through a thorough evaluation for effectiveness. What steps would you take to evaluate this program? Describe them in detail, providing specific examples.

• How would you discipline an employee who has repeatedly reported to work late for a given month (consider the fact that his explanations for his lateness are nonexistent or unsubstantiated)?

- If Jerry is continually late to work, although he may have a viable excuse in that his mother, whom he cares for on a daily basis, is quite ill, then his absence nevertheless has consequences for an orderly administration of the school day. Practically, his class needs coverage. Legal mandates require that students be supervised by licensed personnel. An added complication is that his students are losing out on valuable instructional time by his repeated tardiness or absences. Here's a case in which the organization requires adherence to standard procedures of operation (i.e., attendance policy), yet there are individual constraints (Jerry's need to care for his mother). As principal, you have to make a decision or take a course of action to address this problem. How would you handle this situation?

- How would you begin a process of firing a tenured teacher who verbally abuses his students (consider that you have complaints from parents and students, but you have never seen him behave this way)?

- A rumor spreads in your school that you are resigning. What steps would you take to dispel such rumors?

- A middle school student demands to take his medicine even though no parental consent form is on file, and the parent is unavailable. What would you do?

- Your secretary informs you that she just received a phone call from an anonymous caller saying a bomb will go off in 30 minutes. What do you do?

- Parents and community members complain that your school has no access for people in wheelchairs. They demand that you take action. What would or could you do?

- You discover that some equipment received last month (two VCRs and three DVDs) is missing. What do you do?

- What would you do to encourage teachers to trust that you are there to "help" them and not merely to "evaluate" them?

- How would you forge a role for yourself as an instructional leader and not merely a manager, especially in a school in which the former principal did not focus on instruction?

• How would you maximize all internal and external resources to maximize student learning in your school?

• What procedures and guidelines would you establish with the police and fire departments?

• How will you ensure that the school physical plant, equipment, and support systems are operating safely, efficiently, and effectively?

• There's no homework policy in your school. What steps would you take to establish a policy?

• You are a newly appointed principal who has been notified by the superintendent that each school must establish its own art education program. The superintendent wants you to establish and evaluate the program's effectiveness and to provide a full implementation plan within three months. Describe the steps you would take to establish and evaluate the program. Be sure to include goals and objectives, staffing considerations, criteria for selection, curriculum issues that need to be addressed, materials and resources needed, and so forth. Be as specific as you can.

• A parent calls you and accuses Mr. Henderson of hitting her child. She demands that you immediately dismiss the teacher. She doesn't like your response and threatens to come up to school to shoot you. What do you do?

• During an outdoor lunch period, a boy sustains a deep cut on his leg and is bleeding profusely. You happen on the scene. Describe in step-by-step fashion what you would do from beginning to end.

• The number of accidents in the school yard at lunchtime has increased dramatically. Indicate two immediate steps you would take for dealing with accidents in the yard. State how each step would contribute to safety in the yard.

• You receive a complaint from parents via the telephone and through letters about the incidence of pediculosis (head lice), which appears to be spreading rapidly throughout the school. Some parents are very angry, because their children become affected again after their condition has been cleared up. State four recommendations for immediate action you would make concerning the problem of pediculosis.

- A food fight breaks out during an indoor lunch lineup. You shout over the loudspeaker to no avail. Three lunch aides have not shown up yet. You are alone in the room with nearly 200 children, and about 15 of them are now throwing food. What do you do?

- A teacher reports that her purse is missing. It is five minutes prior to dismissal. She tells you she intends to strip-search the students. Then she hangs up the phone.

- You catch a custodian drinking alcohol on duty in the basement. What do you do?

- Children are bored during indoor lunch lineups. What varied activities can you plan to keep their attention and minimize misbehavior?

- Two secretaries, Ms. Valasquez and Ms. Haley, are in constant conflict over their duties. Set forth and justify the steps you would take to resolve the situation.

- Teachers in your middle school have complained that the dean awards treats to students sent to his office for disciplinary action. They complain to you that such rewards reinforce student misbehavior. The teachers demand action. What would you do?

- As a middle school principal sitting in your office speaking to a parent, you receive a phone call from a lunchroom aide who informs you: "Please come to the cafeteria as fast as you can. All the students are shouting that the food is terrible, and some are throwing their food and trays on the floor. We can't control them." Describe your immediate and long-term actions.

- As a new principal, you find there is no Standard Procedures Manual in your school. No guidelines ever existed for handling most logistical and administrative matters. Describe the steps you'd take to write such a manual and what you would include in the manual.

- You receive this e-mail from a parent:

  Dear Mr. X,

  My son Douglas is in Ms. Treacher's class. Yesterday, two boys in his class, Sam F. and Richard F., asked him for five dollars on the way home from school. Douglas told them he didn't have any money. They said they would beat him up if he didn't bring them the money today. I am keeping Douglas home until I can be sure of his safety.

  Yours truly,

  Mrs. Jackson

  Describe your actions in detail.

- You have been a successful principal for 10 years. The superintendent calls you one afternoon and asks if you'd serve as a mentor for three new principals. These new principals have no idea how to balance their duties of management with other leadership areas. What suggestions could you offer these new principals? Offer at least 10 suggestions.

- How do you find time to renew yourself?

Resource B

Assessing Your Role in
Operational Leadership

A s the principal, you are compelled to assume leadership for the mundane, yet necessary, parts of the job. Your success as principal is predicated on your ability to deal with managerial imperatives and exigencies while at the same time assuming leadership in other dimensions, including instructional. Are you able to undertake both well? Please complete this questionnaire as a means of self-reflection or analysis in order to assess the extent to which you can deal effectively with this form of leadership. Items on the survey are paired, as you'll see, as a way of assessing your points of view and abilities at the extremes. You realize, of course, that the survey is not scientific, and results therefore should be studied in that light. Please note that your responses are private. Your honest responses to the various items below will serve as reflective tools to assist you in becoming an even better operational leader.

Use the following abbreviations, and jot your response in the margin.

SA = Strongly Agree ("For the most part, yes.")
 A = Agree ("Yes, but . . .")
 D = Disagree ("No, but . . .")
SD = Strongly Disagree ("For the most part, no.")

As principal, I should be able to deal effectively with both the operational and educational aspects of the job.
I really think it's unfair and not even possible to undertake both functions with excellent results.

136

It is not asking too much of a principal to deal with both the operational and educational aspects of the job.

It is asking too much of a principal to deal with both the operational and educational aspects of the job.

I am ready to delegate responsibility to others to help do my job.

I feel I must do it myself, or else it won't get done.

I believe I should personally oversee all phases of operations in my school.

I believe that routine administrative matters should be handled by others who are responsible to the principal, and only special and exceptional matters should be referred to the principal.

I personally plan the school's master schedule.

I delegate that responsibility to my AP.

I do not delegate most administrative or logistical matters to my assistant principal so I can devote most of my time to instructional matters; I handle both equally.

I delegate most administrative or logistical matters to my assistant principal so I can devote most of my time to instructional matters.

I designate room assignments personally.

I give my AP that responsibility.

I ensure that school policies and procedures are in sync with district directives.

I rarely consider district mandates and policies since most often they are irrelevant.

I personally examine student test score data in each major academic area.

I have no time to do so.

I personally examine student attendance and tardiness rates to establish patterns of behavior and to develop strategies for dealing with problems.

I have no time to do so; I delegate that responsibility.

I consult my school board on relevant and important managerial matters.
I rarely bother them with such mundane matters.

I conduct and oversee lunch duty.
I do not conduct lunch duty. I supervise it. My AP is there all the time.

I personally write the school's annual report.
I delegate that responsibility to an AP.

I alert the staff to districtwide programs and new initiatives.
I have no time to do so.

I write thank-you notes to my staff for jobs well done.
I do so only once a year.

I distribute surveys to parents, teachers, staff, and students to ascertain how well my school is managed.
I have never done so.

I work closely with the head custodian to ensure that major work and improvements are concluded in a timely fashion.
Because I have no knowledge of custodial matters, I let the custodian carry on independently, reporting to me occasionally.

I inspect the school building roof.
I never have done so.

I conduct a security walk-through on a daily basis.
Perhaps I do so monthly.

I coordinate all school events, during and after school, with the custodian.
I rarely do so in reality; I have no time.

I check on instructional materials' availability in supply closets.
I have a secretary do that.

I order new textbooks for different grades.
I let teachers or APs do that.

I collect and monitor teacher attendance, grade, and lesson plan
   books.
I rarely do that anymore; who has the time?

If I don't manage my school well, I can't lead effectively.
I can still be an effective leader even though I care little
   about managerial matters, because in the end, they really
   handle themselves.

I am an efficient and effective manager.
I am neither a very efficient nor an effective manager.

I meet all district deadlines for reports, projects, and so on.
I am a procrastinator, and they know it.

I pride myself on my good organizational skills.
I need help in this area.

I have good time management skills.
Time flies by; I have little time to do all that needs to be done.

I deal with stress well, under most circumstances.
I am stressed out most of the time, especially as the day wears on.

I personally evaluate every worker in my building.
Who has the time to do that? I "hit" the main people.

I know how to relax.
I relax on weekends.

I realize that every action I take is seen and being studied by others.
I am unaware or simply don't care what others think.

I take my responsibility to hire and fire seriously.
I have no control over either.

I am the most important person in the school in terms of setting the tone for good pupil behavior.
The teacher is more important than I am.

I am aware of state and federal statutes as they relate to various legal issues facing life in schools (e.g., student searches, sexual harassment, drug testing, school prayer).
I am legally inept.

I maintain eye contact with the person to whom I am speaking.
I can't stand people. I prefer to interact infrequently.

I am familiar with most aspects of school law.
I am somewhat familiar with most aspects of school law.

I conduct fair evaluations of my teachers.
I give everyone a satisfactory grade, because it's impossible to remove an incompetent tenured teacher.

I wouldn't mind if teachers evaluated my work as principal.
They have no right to evaluate me; I'm the boss.

I am good at managing conflict among staff members.
I let people work out their own issues.

I take my role as manager seriously.
I prefer to focus exclusively on nonmanagerial duties.

Although I am a manager, I realize that role is insufficient. In order to be effective, I must lead effectively as well.
Although I am a leader, I realize that role is insufficient. In order to be effective, I must manage effectively as well.

I personally oversee the program to induct and mentor new teachers.
Who has the time? My APs assist.

I am the only true leader in the building.
Everyone can lead in different ways.

I am responsible for all budgetary items in my school.
I wish I had no responsibility for budget.

I should be held accountable for any serious budgetary errors.
The superintendent or central office should be accountable; I'm
    too busy.

I develop and oversee the school's strategic financial plan.
My AP does that.

I ensure that transportation procedures for students in my school
    are well established.
My AP ensures that transportation procedures for students in my
    school are well established.

I am well organized.
I am generally disorganized, but that is OK because I have an AP
    who is very well organized.

I keep an orderly office.
My office is a mess, and I prefer it that way.

I am generally on top of things.
I am generally lost when it comes to managerial matters.

I rely only on myself.
I tend to rely on others, too.

It is indeed possible to be a great manager and a great leader.
It's impossible, and anyone who tells you it is possible is lying.

You cannot serve as an effective leader without needing to attend
    to managerial matters.
You can serve as an effective leader without needing to attend too
    much to managerial matters.

I am conversant with all standard operational procedures in my
    school building.
I rarely, if ever, refer to that manual.

I would not hesitate to ask a colleague or my superintendent for
   advice regarding managing my school.
To be honest, I would be embarrassed to do that.

I oversee fire drills in my school.
My AP does that, too.

I keep an eye on the exterior of my school building to ensure
   there's no graffiti or physical damage present.
I rarely do that, because that should be the custodian's job.

I monitor hallway and bulletin board displays.
My AP does that; I have no time, because I am usually spending
   time completing reports for the district office.

I am an effective communicator to all community constituents.
I don't communicate well; I prefer to manage from my office.

I review supply inventories for my school.
I never do; my secretary handles those matters.

I balance my professional and personal lives well.
I am a workaholic, and I rarely get a chance to care for myself.

I am able to prioritize tasks well.
I get overwhelmed easily, so I take one task on at a time.

I need no help managing my school.
I can use a mentor.

I'm a very good manager, but a poor instructional leader.
I am a good instructional leader, but quite a disorganized
   manager.

I work well in chaos.
I just can't stand disruptions.

I use technology to help me organize managerial tasks in school.
I shy away from technology.

I can use technology in all its facets.
Aside from e-mail, I really don't feel comfortable with much technology.

People usually understand me.
People seem to continually misinterpret my motives.

I rarely get angry.
I get angry frequently.

I am a good listener.
I am a poor listener.

I am laid-back and easygoing. Managing my school is relatively easy.
I am nervous over most managerial functions and matters.

I delegate just enough.
I delegate too much.

I label documents carefully before I put them away.
I rarely file anything; my secretary does most of it.

I can locate my paperwork easily.
Papers usually get lost.

I complete most projects in a timely manner.
Time seems to fly, and I rarely complete my projects on time.

I am a self-starter.
It's hard to motivate myself at times.

I have enough principal colleagues I can confide in.
I am a loner and prefer it that way.

When an incident occurs, I usually put it in writing as a form of documentation for possible later use.
I usually forget to document such matters.

I meticulously keep anecdotals.
I rarely record information myself or keep anecdotals.

Evaluation is necessary to ensure accountability.
I have little time, so I give everyone a satisfactory grade.

Evaluation and supervision accomplish the same goal.
They are different functions.

I manage conflict well.
I avoid conflict at all costs.

I am in touch with the local fire department on a regular basis.
Who has the time? I think I contacted them once in two years.

I communicate with local politicians as necessary regarding issues
    affecting my school.
Who has the time?

I oversee all fire drills and provide appropriate training to the
    entire staff.
My AP does.

I review child abuse laws and regulations with my staff.
I don't do so, because they all know about these regulations
    already.

I oversee all equipment inventory in my school.
Who has the time? My AP handles this for me.

I take pride in my managerial duties as principal.
I hate my managerial duties.

I don't let my managerial responsibilities detract from leadership
    imperatives.
They often do, though.

I am able to handle both managing and leading my school with facility and ease.
I can't seem to get a handle on both functions.

I oversee all major purchases in my school.
My secretary does that for me; who has the time?

I carefully monitor all budgetary items on my own.
I delegate budget to my secretary, and she notifies me if anything major is needed.

Although I delegate budget to my assistant, I oversee all expenditures and related budgetary items.
I delegate it all to my AP.

Well-established procedures exist for supply and equipment requisitions.
I rarely have the time to monitor supply and equipment requisitions.

I handle all inventorying myself.
I delegate and oversee inventorying.

I consult my faculty and staff before I purchase major instructional or other items.
I don't bother them with administrative tasks.

I have had my school checked for asbestos.
Oops.

My planned budget reflects the priorities for the school.
I put together my budget regardless of school priorities, because there are items that transcend our goals and objectives.

I never make plans unless I consider school budget and resource allocation.
I rarely consider school budget and resource allocation when planning.

I am ready to reallocate current resources, if needed, to reach our strategic goals.
Once the budget is set, I will not make any changes.

I provide for accountability of a budget tied to student outcomes.
I rarely consider student outcomes when it comes to budgeting.

Whenever we make copies, use postage, or repair audiovisual aids, I keep budgetary constraints in mind.
I never do so.

I try to follow these steps in the budget process: Review budget data and standard operational procedures; tie budget to student learning; create a draft budget; share draft budget, collect feedback, and prepare final draft; implement budget; receive feedback on budget.
I rarely do so.

I have a plan for inspecting the school plant and all facilities.
I have too much to do to inspect facilities. I have the custodian do so, and then I consult with him or her as needed.

I regularly evaluate maintenance of my building.
I have no time to manage maintenance of my building, because I focus on instructional leadership.

Written guidelines for safety exist in my school.
I have no idea if written guidelines exist, but I talk about safety to all students.

I open the school building each morning.
The custodian is responsible for opening and closing the school building.

I am precisely aware of how my building is utilized on a daily basis.
I let my custodian and one of my APs discuss building utilization.

I see no connection between the physical aspects of the school plant and student achievement.
I believe that the physical aspects of the school plant and its maintenance contribute to overall school climate, which influences student achievement, albeit indirectly.

I evaluate the effectiveness of main office procedures regularly.
My secretary monitors all office stuff; I'm too busy.

I have a system in place to evaluate secretarial and clerical personnel.
I have no system in place.

My office staff is familiar and conversant with the latest technologies.
They don't even use e-mail.

I train all office staff on how to answer the phone and how to
     converse with visitors or school guests.
I don't have to, because they usually do the right thing.

We have a master calendar posted in the main office.
No master calendar exists.

I conduct regular meetings with all office staff.
I have no time for such meetings.

All school records and important reports are kept confidential.
I never thought about that.

I am familiar with basic budgetary procedures in my district.
I'm clueless, but it doesn't affect my work in the school.

I oversee and evaluate food services in my school.
I have no time to do so. They have their own supervisor.

I write clear memoranda.
I write too many memoranda.

I use e-mail as an important method of communicating.
I e-mail people too much, or so they tell me.

I have a copy of state codes of governance.
I know of no such codes.

I understand the district budget cycle.
I don't even know if one exists.

I oversee faculty and student books and instructional supply distribution.
My secretary or AP does that.

I am aware of varied furniture needs of my faculty.
My secretary or AP does that.

I know how to handle grievance hearings.
I can't seem to keep up with all those regulations.

I have thoroughly read the district's Standard Operations Procedures Manual and keep it handy as a reference guide.
Does one exist?

I provide training for staff regarding procedures to follow during health emergencies.
I provide no such training.

My school has developed an emergency plan, and it is reviewed regularly.
I have never developed such a plan, or I did develop one but have never enforced it.

Student accident reports are completed and filed appropriately and in a timely fashion.
I rarely check if they are completed and filed properly.

I regularly evaluate school plant and facilities using a formal evaluation form developed by the district or self-developed.
I do not do so.

I am conversant with city or town health codes and can spot violations when they occur.
I cannot.

I occasionally review collective bargaining agreements.
I rarely do so.

In general, I manage time well.
I am overwhelmed . . . ugh.

I can coordinate a schoolwide discipline plan.
I delegate these duties to my APs.

I was fully prepared to coordinate lunch duty before I became a
    principal.
I was not fully prepared to coordinate lunch duty before I became
    a principal.

I should be responsible for overseeing the school safety plan.
Someone from the central office should, but not me, because I'm
    too busy.

It's always good to have taken course work to help prepare for
    management exigencies, even though we learn best on the
    job.
All management issues can be learned on the job.

Analyze your responses:

Pair with a colleague and share your responses to each paired item. Be honest with yourself. What did you learn from the exercise?

Resource C

An Annotated Bibliography
of Best Resources

T he literature on the principalship and related areas is extensive. The list below is not meant to serve as a comprehensive resource by any means. The selected titles I have annotated are few, but in my opinion, they are among the most useful references on the subject. Rather than "impress" you with a more extensive list, I have selected these outstanding works related to operational leadership that will supplement my book quite well. I may have missed, of course, other important works. Nevertheless, the list below is a good start. Don't forget that life is a long journey of continuous learning. Continue to hone your skills by reading good books and journal articles on operational leadership. No one is ever perfect, and everyone can learn something new by keeping current with the literature in the field. Share your readings and reactions with a colleague.

Fiscal Management

Garner, C. W. (2004). *Education finance for school leaders: Strategic planning and administration.* Upper Saddle River, NJ: Pearson/Merrill Prentice Hall.

Textbook on school finance, yet highly readable and very detailed.

Ramsey, R. D. (2001). *Fiscal fitness for school administrators: How to stretch resources and do even more with less.* Thousand Oaks, CA: Corwin.

Sometimes, more likely often, fiscal issues frighten many prospective or beginning principals. This book is a great resource—easy to follow yet comprehensive.

Getting Organized

Simon, R. A., & Newman, J. F. (2004). *Making time to lead: How principals can stay on top of it all.* Thousand Oaks, CA: Corwin.

Practical and very easy-to-read manual with excellent, field-tested strategies for organizing and for dealing with time, communication, and more management-related requirements.

Operational Management

Bolman, L. G., & Deal, T. E. (2003). *Reframing organizations: Artistry, choice, and leadership* (3rd ed.). San Francisco: Jossey-Bass.

If there is one book to read, this is the one! A classic. Pay careful attention to discussion of both the structural and human resources frame. The most insightful treatments into how organizations work. A must-read.

Brock, B. L., & Grady, M. L. (2004). *Launching your first principalship: A guide for beginning principals.* Thousand Oaks, CA: Corwin.

Packed with practical, easy-to-use suggestions, especially if you are beginning your career as a principal. Chapters are short, so you can read a chapter an evening or one a weekend. Enjoyable and practical.

Fuller, G. (1990). *Supervisor's portable answer book.* Englewood Cliffs, NJ: Prentice Hall.

A must-read. Not for principals exclusively, but this highly readable, even enjoyable manual is packed with questions and thoughtful and practical answers to problems we face in our job. Among the most useful topics included are: How to Master Commonsense Communication; Successfully Supervising Difficult People; The Art of Overcoming Employee Complaints; The Do's and Don'ts of Dishing out Discipline; The In's and Out's of Hiring and Firing; and Problems You Don't Want—But Can't Avoid.

Jones, J. (2005). *Management skills in schools: A resource for school leaders.* London: Paul Chapman.

A comprehensive yet readable treatment that covers many topics in this book. Easy-to-read and useful strategies offered.

Knoll, M. (1984). *Elementary principal's survival guide: Practical techniques and materials for day-to-day school administration and supervision.* Englewood Cliffs, NJ: Prentice Hall.

Dated, but still useful, guide to a variety of essential management imperatives. Clearly laid out and very easy to read (a large book, not in length but in size), this book covers such practical topics as preparing for fire drills, handling accidents, creating schedules, monitoring attendance records, beautifying the building, selecting instructional materials, developing budget plans, hiring substitute teachers, and much more. Also, for a similar useful survival manual for the high school, see *Secondary Principal's Survival Guide: Practical Techniques and Materials for Successful School Administration* by Robert D. Ramsey (Prentice Hall, 1992).

Kosmoski, G. J., & Pollack, D. R. (2005). *Managing difficult, frustrating, and hostile conversations: Strategies for savvy administrators* (2nd ed.). Thousand Oaks, CA: Corwin.

Serving as a principal is usually a joy. Sometimes, however, we are confronted with seemingly intractable problems that test our nerves and will. This brief yet extremely practical book is packed with strategies for dealing with those unfortunate problems we may confront. Topics include dealing with aggressive personalities, embarrassing situations, and complainers and combating charges of discrimination.

Shaver, H. (2004). *Organize, communicate, empower: How principals can make time for leadership.* Thousand Oaks, CA: Corwin.

Short, yet packed with practical, easy-to-read and -use strategies. Contents will equip you with a variety of techniques to handle many logistical and managerial duties.

Miscellaneous Management-Related Issues

Black, J. A., & English, F. W. (1986). *What they don't tell you in schools of education about school administration.* Lancaster, PA: Technomic.

Classic treatise for coping with school politics—includes career suggestions and a host of other topics; a must-read; a classic.

Blanchard, K., & Johnson, S. (1984). *The one-minute manager.* New York: William Morrow.

Short and a must-read.

Buckingham, M. (2005). *The one thing you need to know about great managing, great leading, and sustained individual success.* New York: Free Press.

Not just the latest how-to book, but a sensible, thorough, and realistic treatment of management in contrast to leadership. An enjoyable read that will help you focus your own efforts and at the same time will give you more in-depth understanding of others.

Drake, T. L., & Roe, W. H. (2003). *The principalship* (6th ed.). Upper Saddle River, NJ: Merrill Prentice Hall.

Textbooky, but packed with information. Intelligently written and comprehensive.

Koehler, M. (1999). *Administrator's staff development activities kit.* San Francisco: Jossey-Bass.

Ready-to-use teaching materials for training, supervision, and evaluation; reproducible forms; great for inservice.

Mamchak, P. S., & Mamchak, S. R. (1998). *Encyclopedia of school letters.* San Francisco: Jossey-Bass.

Packed with sample memos and letters in many areas principals would need.

Meyer, H. E. (1992). *Lifetime encyclopedia of letters.* Englewood Cliffs, NJ: Prentice Hall.

Valuable resource to write letters that do the following: requesting favors, declining requests, fund-raising, providing info, dealing with complaints, expressing sympathy and condolences, offering congratulations, and so forth.

Owings, W. A., & Kaplan, L. S. (2003). *Best practices, best thinking, and emerging issues in school leadership.* Thousand Oaks, CA: Corwin.

Excellent resource to keep abreast of trends and issues in educational leadership and management dealing with issues of accountability, special education, technology, and school law, among many others.

Ramsey, R. D. (1996). *The principal's book of lists.* San Francisco: Jossey-Bass.

Useful lists; a nuts-and-bolts book with lots of information, tips, and so on.

Senge, P. (1990). *The fifth discipline: The art and practice of the learning organization.* New York: Doubleday.

A classic to read and reread.

Personal Development

Covey, S. R. (1989). *The 7 habits of highly effective people.* New York: Simon & Schuster.

A classic; a must-read and -reread.

Glanz, J. (2000). *Relax for success: A practical guide for educators to relieve stress.* Norwood, MA: Christopher-Gordon.

Useful resource for dealing with stress—comes with a CD-ROM.

Queen, J. A., & Queen, P. S. (2005). *The frazzled principal's wellness plan: Reclaiming time, managing stress, and creating a healthy lifestyle.* Thousand Oaks, CA: Corwin.

> The title says it all; highly recommended; a fast, enjoyable read.

Seligman, M. (1998). *Learned optimism.* New York: Free Press.

> Definitely one of the best books I ever read that helped me gain a fresh perspective on work and life; a classic in the field.

School Law

Dunklee, D. R., & Shoop, R. J. (2006). *The principal's quick-reference guide to school law: Reducing liability, litigation, and other potential legal tangles* (2nd ed.). Thousand Oaks, CA: Corwin.

> One of the most comprehensive yet easy-to-read and -manage books on the topic. Quite honestly, most works on law turn me off, because I am not a lawyer type. This book, however, is different. It is a must-read reference work. It translates all that we learned and forgot in the law course we took in grad school into practical, easy-to-remember guidelines. If there were only one book to read on school law, this would be the book I'd recommend.

Best Web Sites for Principals

Conduct a search, because many more exist, of course; e.g., type in "principals" on www.google.com.

http://www.cybertext.net.au/tct2002/tutorials/section5.htm—Offers many links for school leaders

http://nt.watauga.k12.nc.us/whs/wonders/admin.htm—Nice Web site for school administrators

http://www.aasa.org/—American Association of School Administrators

http://www.naesp.org/—National Association of Elementary School Principals

http://www.nassp.org/—National Association of Secondary School Principals

http://www.principals.org—Loads of information and valuable links

www.ed.gov—The U.S. Department of Education Web site

www.teachers.net/lessons/search.html—This site enables you to search for a lesson plan for K–12

www.teachers.net/cgi-bin/lessons/sort.cgi—Lesson plans at this site are sorted by category

www.glavac.com—Busy educator's guide to the World Wide Web

www.k-6educators.about.com—Offers links for elementary educators

www.yahoo.com/Education/K_12—Offers links to reference materials

www.new-teacher.com—A site for new teachers and student teachers

www.discoveryschool.com/schrockguide—Kathy Schrock's Guide for Educators is a categorized list of sites on the Internet (updated daily) found to be useful for enhancing curriculum and teacher professional growth

www.teachernet.com—Smart ideas for busy teachers

www.AtoZteacherstuff.com—Online lesson plans

www.NAEYC.org—National Association for the Education of Young Children

www.google.com—Great advice: search Google by typing in "school management"—now, spend the day exploring. (Also, try typing in "discipline," although many nonschool discipline sites are included, so you'll have to pick and choose. It's worth exploring, though. Google is most accessible, easy to use, and current.)

www.masterteacher.com—This for-profit Web site is a phenomenal storehouse of educational resources (some for free) that includes videos, books on a host of relevant topics (e.g., leadership, inclusion, mentoring). It is a must to browse, with loads of teaching ideas. Great free catalog; subscribe for free materials at 800-669-9633

http://soupserver.com—Daily inspirational sayings; uplifts the soul

www.newteachercenter.org—Promotes excellence and diversity in schools—very teacher friendly

www.alfiekohn.org—Useful site packed with the ideas and writings of a noted critic of public education

www.effectiveteaching.com—Harry Wong's site packed with info

www.pdkintl.org—National organization of immense influence

www.proteacher.com and www.innovativeclassroom.com—Both sites contain many useful ideas and tools (including lesson plans in content areas) on a variety of educational topics; easy to navigate

www.splcenter.org—Tolerance and diversity issues

www.ascd.org—Great resources on a plethora of topics

www.school.discovery.com/schrockguide/assess.html—An impressive list of resources related to assessment

www.lessonplanspage.com—More than 1,000 lesson plans for K–12

www.askeric.org/virtual/lessons—Lesson plans by topic and grade level

Consult the ASCD journal *Educational Leadership*'s "Web Wonders" column. Also, see Susan Brooks-Young's *101 Best Web Sites for Principals* (Eugene, OR: International Society for Technology in Education, 2003).

References

Alvy, H., & Robbins, P. (1998). *If I only knew: Success strategies for navigating the principalship.* Thousand Oaks, CA: Corwin.

Alvy, H., & Robbins, P. (2005). Growing into leadership. *Educational Leadership, 62*(8), 50–54.

Bennis, W. G. (1990). *Why leaders can't lead: The unconscious conspiracy continues.* San Francisco: Jossey-Bass.

Bolman, L. G., & Deal, T. E. (2000). People and organizations. In M. Fullan (Ed.), *The Jossey-Bass reader on: Educational leadership* (pp. 59–69). San Francisco: Jossey-Bass.

Bolton, R. (1986). *People skills.* New York: Touchstone.

Brock, B. L., & Grady, M. L. (2004). *Launching your first principalship: A guide for beginning principals.* Thousand Oaks, CA: Corwin.

Cotton, K. (2003). *Principals and student achievement: What research says.* Alexandria, VA: Association for Supervision and Curriculum Development.

Daresh, J. C. (2001). *Beginning the principalship: A practical guide for new school leaders* (2nd ed.). Thousand Oaks, CA: Corwin.

Davies, B. (Ed.). (2005). *The essentials of school leadership.* London: Paul Chapman Publishing and Corwin.

Deming, W. E. (2000). *Out of the crisis.* Cambridge: MIT Press.

DeRoche, E. F. (1987). *An administrator's guide for evaluating programs and personnel: An effective schools approach* (2nd ed.). Boston: Allyn & Bacon.

Drake, T. L., & Roe, W. H. (2003). *The principalship* (6th ed.). Upper Saddle River, NJ: Merrill Prentice Hall.

Dunklee, D. R., & Shoop, R. J. (2006). *The principal's quick-reference guide to school law: Reducing liability, litigation, and other potential legal tangles* (2nd ed.). Thousand Oaks, CA: Corwin.

Elmore, R. F. (1990). *Restructuring schools: The next generation of educational reform.* San Francisco: Jossey-Bass.

Fayol, H. (1916). *General and industrial management.* London: Pittman.

Feigelson, S. (1998). *Energize your meetings with laughter.* Alexandria, VA: Association for Supervision and Curriculum Development.

Garner, C. W. (2004). *Education finance for school leaders: Strategic planning and administration.* Upper Saddle River, NJ: Pearson/Merrill Prentice Hall.

Ginott, H. (1993). *Teacher and child: A book for parents and teachers.* New York: Macmillan.

Glanz, J. (1994). Redefining the roles and responsibilities of assistant principals. *Clearing House, 67,* 283–288.

Glanz, J. (2000). *Relax for success: A practical guide for educators to relieve stress.* Norwood, MA: Christopher-Gordon.

Glanz, J. (2004). *The assistant principal's handbook.* Thousand Oaks, CA: Corwin.

Green, R. L. (2005). *Practicing the art of leadership: A problem-based approach to implementing the ISLLC standards* (2nd ed.). Upper Saddle River, NJ: Pearson/Merrill Prentice Hall.

Hersey, P., & Blanchard, K. (1992). *Management of organizational behavior* (6th ed.). Englewood Cliffs, NJ: Prentice Hall.

Kaser, J., Mundry, S., Loucks-Horsley, S., & Stiles, K. E. (2002). *Leading every day: 124 actions to effective leadership.* Thousand Oaks, CA: Corwin.

Keil, V. L. (2005). Communicating for results. *Principal Leadership, 5*(8), 28–31.

Kerlinger, F. N. (1986). *Foundations of behavioral research* (3rd ed.). San Diego, CA: Harcourt Brace.

Lunenburg, F. C., & Ornstein, A. C. (1996). *Educational administration: Concepts and practices* (2nd ed.). Belmont, CA: Wadsworth.

Marzano, R. J. (2003). *What works in schools: Translating research into action.* Alexandria, VA: Association for Supervision and Curriculum Development.

Maslow, A. H. (1954). *Motivation and personality.* New York: Harper & Row.

Matthews, L. J., & Crow, G. M. (2003). *Being and becoming a principal: Role conceptions for contemporary principals and assistant principals.* Boston: Allyn & Bacon.

Mayhew, K. C., & Edwards, A. C. (1965). *The Dewey school: The Laboratory School of the University of Chicago, 1896–1903.* New York: Atherton Press.

McGregor, D. (1960). *The human side of enterprise.* New York: McGraw-Hill.

Northouse, P. G. (1997). *Leadership: Theory and practice.* Thousand Oaks, CA: Sage.

Oplatka, I. (2005). The principal's career stage: An absent element in leadership perspectives. *International Journal of Leadership in Education, 7*(1), 43–55.

Osterman, K. F., & Kottkamp, R. B. (2004). *Reflective practice for educators* (2nd ed.). Thousand Oaks, CA: Corwin.

Ramsey, R. D. (2001). *Fiscal fitness for school administrators.* Thousand Oaks, CA: Corwin.

Sanders, J. R. (2000). *Evaluating school programs: An educator's guide.* Thousand Oaks, CA: Corwin.

Senge, P. (1990). *The fifth discipline.* New York: Doubleday.

Sergiovanni, T. J. (2000). *Leadership for the schoolhouse.* San Francisco: Jossey-Bass.

Simon, R. A., & Newman, J. F. (2004). *Making time to lead: How principals can stay on top of it all.* Thousand Oaks, CA: Corwin.

Sullivan, S., & Glanz, J. (2005). *Supervision that improves teaching: Strategies and techniques* (2nd ed.). Thousand Oaks, CA: Corwin.

Sullivan, S., & Glanz, J. (2006). *Building effective learning communities: Strategies for leadership, learning, & collaboration.* Thousand Oaks, CA: Corwin.

Ubben, G. C., Hughes, L. W., & Norris, C. J. (2004). *The principal: Creative leadership for excellence in schools.* Boston: Allyn & Bacon.

Wilmore, E. L. (2002). *Principal leadership: Applying the new Educational Leadership Constituent Council (ELCC) standards.* Thousand Oaks, CA: Corwin.

Young, P. G. (2004). *You have to go to school—You're the principal: 101 tips to make it better for your students, your staff, and yourself.* Thousand Oaks, CA: Corwin.

Index

Note: Pages marked with a *t* are tables; those marked with an *f* are figures.

**CORWIN
PRESS**

The Corwin Press logo—a raven striding across an open book—represents the union of courage and learning. Corwin Press is committed to improving education for all learners by publishing books and other professional development resources for those serving the field of PreK–12 education. By providing practical, hands-on materials, Corwin Press continues to carry out the promise of its motto: **"Helping Educators Do Their Work Better."**